iBooks Author

FOR

DUMMIES®

by Galen Gruman

WILEY

John Wiley & Sons, Inc.

iBooks® Author For Dummies®

Published by
John Wiley & Sons, Inc.
111 River Street
Hoboken, NJ 07030-5774
www.wiley.com

WILEY

About the Author

Galen Gruman has been doing production of newspapers, magazines, and books for about 35 years, having caught the layout and production bug from his junior high school newspaper. He was involved in one of the first desktop publishing efforts of a national publication in the early 1980s and has reviewed desktop publishing software for both *InfoWorld* (IDG Enterprise) and *Macworld* (Mac Publishing) until the late 1990s. Since 1990, he's co-authored or written a series of how-to books for the publisher of this book, John Wiley & Sons, for most of the major layout programs of their eras: PageMaker, QuarkXPress, and InDesign. Gruman has also been doing some website coding and production over the last decade and has produced e-books for Wiley in the more recent years, in addition to his day job as the InfoWorld.com website's executive editor. iBooks Author represents the next wave of publishing, so of course he had to learn — and teach — this tool, as well.

Publisher's Acknowledgments

We're proud of this book; please send us your comments at http://dummies.custhelp.com. For other comments, please contact our Customer Care Department within the U.S. at 877-762-2974, outside the U.S. at 317-572-3993, or fax 317-572-4002.

Some of the people who helped bring this book to market include the following:

Acquisitions and Editorial

Project Editor: Laura K. Miller

Acquisitions Editor: Kyle Looper

Copy Editor: Laura K. Miller

Technical Editor: Dennis R. Cohen

Editorial Manager: Jodi Jensen

Editorial Assistant: Leslie Saxman

Sr. Editorial Assistant: Cherie Case

Cover Photo: © iStockphoto.com / ALEAIMAGE © iStockphoto.com / marinello

Interior Photos: Courtesy of Ingall W. Bulls, III

Composition Services

Project Coordinator: Kristie Rees

Layout and Graphics: Joyce Haughey, Christin Swinford

Proofreader: Sossity R. Smith

Indexer: Valerie Haynes Perry

Publishing and Editorial for Technology Dummies

    Richard Swadley, Vice President and Executive Group Publisher

    Andy Cummings, Vice President and Publisher

    Mary Bednarek, Executive Acquisitions Director

    Mary C. Corder, Editorial Director

Publishing for Consumer Dummies

    Kathleen Nebenhaus, Vice President and Executive Publisher

Composition Services

    Debbie Stailey, Director of Composition Services

Table of Contents

Introduction

An e-book is no longer just a book you read on a computer, tablet, smartphone, or e-reader. Thanks to Apple's iBooks Author software, an e-book can be a dynamic experience, letting readers explore information through interactive graphics, audio and video recordings, slideshow presentations, and live web widgets (a snippet of web functionality, not a full website or web page).

Imagine children's books that let readers explore the story and connect with other fans. Imagine a service manual that lets a technician get the most recent parts information and turn a 3D diagram around to get a better understanding of a potentially malfunctioning part. Imagine a financial report, a scientific paper, a how-to book, an encyclopedia, a documentary-style history book, or any other document exploring complex and changing information that could go beyond text and static images.

You don't have to imagine such documents any longer. You can create them instead on your Mac with Apple's free iBooks Author software and distribute them — for free or for money — to any iPad user, of which there are tens of millions.

But iBooks Author is a first-version product, and that lack of maturity clearly shows in some of the limitations and unintuitive approaches it has when it comes to creating that new kind of dynamic publication that makes iBooks Author so compelling. So users may need a guide to not just the possibilities, but also how to deal with the potholes in the road along the way.

What This Book Offers

This book explains how to create dynamic documents in iBooks Author, as well as how to distribute them to readers. You don't need to be a book publisher to use iBooks Author, thanks to its straightforward user interface; if you've used Apple's Pages word processor, you already know how to use many of iBooks Author's textual and layout capabilities.

Of course, the more you know about creating the interactive elements iBooks Author can embed in your e-book, the more advantage you can take of iBooks Author in your own project. The good news is that you can use none, some, or all of these dynamic features in your iBooks Author e-book, so you can start with what you already know and build up skills in the other areas over time, as needed.

This book won't teach you how to create videos, websites, slide-shows, or 3D graphics. You need to use the appropriate tools for each of those, which I point you to in the following section.

This book does explain how to prepare your content for use in iBooks Author, lay out an e-book optimally for reading on the iPad, and distribute your e-book to iPad users.

What You Need to Use iBooks Author

iBooks Author is available only for Macintosh computers, so you must have a Mac to use it. And not just any Mac: iBooks Author requires that your Mac run Mac OS X Lion version 10.7.2 or later (or the Mac OS X Mountain Lion version 10.8, to be released in summer 2012), which means your Mac must use an Intel chip. The free iBooks Author application is available only through the Apple Mac App Store, which you access via the App Store software that comes with Mac OS X Lion (and OS X Mountain Lion).

iBooks Author's Mac orientation isn't limited to needing a Mac to run it. If you want to embed a slideshow, you must create them in Apple's Keynote software, available for $10 on the iPad and for $20 on the Mac. (You can also get Keynote as part of the Apple $79 iWork suite sold in some online and physical retail stories on discs.)

Of course, you need the tools to create your source files. For text created outside iBooks Author, you're limited to Microsoft Word (or programs that can export to the Word .doc or .docx format) and Apple Pages. For tables, you're limited to Word, Excel, Pages, and Numbers. Note that iBooks Author doesn't care if the files were created on a Mac or Windows PC (or, in the case of Pages and Numbers, on a Mac or iPad). And for web widgets, you're limited to Apple's Dashcode and Tumult's Hype applications, although you can always link to an external website (which opens in the iPad's Safari browser) from your iBooks Author e-book.

For the other supported file types — PDFs, graphics, audio, and video — you can use any programs that produce the compat-ible file formats. Examples include Adobe's Creative Suite and its individual components (such as Photoshop for graphics, Acrobat Pro for PDFs, and Premiere for video), Apple GarageBand for audio, Apple Final Cut and iMovie for video, Mac OS X's included QuickTime Pro for audio and video (including screencasts), and Collada-supporting apps such as Photoshop, Google Sketchup Pro, and Strata 3D for 3D images. (Chapters 4 and 6 explain the supported file formats in detail.)

You also need an iPad. Well, strictly speaking, you don't need an iPad because you can preview your e-book on the Mac, but realistically, you want an iPad to test your e-books in the actual environment in which they'll be used. Any model will do; the free iBooks 2.0 (or later) application that supports the iBooks Author format runs on all versions of the iPad, as long as you have the current (iOS 5 or later) operating system installed. (Your readers thus also need iPads running iOS 5 and iBooks 2.0, or later versions.)

To distribute e-books through Apple's online iBookstore requires that you have a publisher's account with Apple, and if you want to charge money for your e-book, you need access to a service that provides the ISBN codes booksellers must use for each book. (Chapter 8 explains how to set up a publisher's account and how to get ISBN codes.)

Conventions Used in This Book

Throughout this book, I describe how to use the mouse and keyboard shortcuts for many of the applications covered. In doing so, I use the terms in the following sections to explain mouse, trackpad, and keyboard actions.

Mouse and trackpad conventions

I ask you to use your mouse or trackpad to run your Mac and all the applications that help you get work done. When I do, I use the following terms:

✔ **Click:** Most Mac mice have only one button, but some have two or more. If you have a multi-button mouse, quickly press and release the leftmost mouse button once when I say to click the mouse. On an Apple Mighty Mouse or Magic Mouse, click the left side of the top surface. (For other mice that have only one button, just press and release the button you have.) If you're using a MacBook laptop or Magic Trackpad, click the trackpad.

✔ **Double-click:** When I say to double-click, quickly press and release the leftmost mouse button twice (if your mouse has only one button, just press and release twice the button you have). On some multi-button mice, one of the buttons can function as a double-click (you click it once, the mouse clicks twice); if your mouse has this feature, use it — it saves strain on your hand. You can also double-click a trackpad.

✔ **Right-click:** Right-clicking means clicking the right mouse button. (With an Apple Mighty Mouse or Magic Mouse, you can click the right side of the top surface to get a right-click; just be sure to enable that capability in the Mouse system preference.) On a Mac's one-button mouse, hold the Control key when clicking the mouse button to achieve the right-click effect. On multi-button Mac mice, Mac OS X automatically assigns the right button to Control-click. On a MacBook's trackpad, hold the Control key when clicking the trackpad. Newer MacBooks and the Magic Trackpad can also be con-figured to right-click by tapping the lower-right corner of the trackpad or tapping with two fingers.

✔ **Drag:** Dragging is used for moving and sizing items in a docu-ment. To drag an item, position the mouse pointer on it. Press and hold the mouse button, and then slide the mouse across a flat surface to drag the item. Release the mouse button to drop the dragged item in its new location. You can also drag by using the trackpad in the same fashion.

Menu commands

The commands that you select by using the program menus appear in this book in normal typeface.

Mac OS X has several kinds of menus:

✔ **Menus:** All Mac OS X applications, including the Finder, display their main menu options at the top of the screen, in OS X's menu bar. Click a menu heading to see its menu options, and click the desired menu option to choose it.

✔ **Pop-up menus:** Within an application's dialog boxes, panels, toolbars, and other user-interface elements, you may see menus indicated by a set of triangles (one pointing up and one pointing down) or a single down-pointing triangle. (Technically, those with the down-pointing triangle are called *pull-down menus,* but for simplicity, I call them all pop-up menus because they all work the same way.) Such pop-up menus have several presentation styles:

- Displayed in a rounded rectangle

- Have a name or icon with the menu indicator (the tri-angle icon) to its right

- Have their options in a white box (which means they're fields whose options you can simply enter yourself, such as a font name, rather than use the menu options)

Pop-up menus that use icons rather than text labels are called *icon menus*. Click a pop-up menu to see its menu options, and click the desired menu option to choose it.

✔ **Contextual menus:** Some menus are invisible until you right-click or Control-click an object on the screen. A menu of options appears next to where you right-clicked or Control-clicked; click the desired menu option to choose it.

If no contextual menu appears, it means that particular object has no options or that you have to use some other means (such as a dialog box or panel) to apply options to that object.

When you choose some menu commands, a related submenu appears with additional options. You can tell that a menu option has such a submenu because a right-facing triangle appears to the far left of the menu option's name or icon.

If I describe a situation in which you need to select one menu and then choose a command from a secondary menu or list box, I use an arrow symbol. For example, if I tell you to choose Edit⇨Paste, you choose the Paste menu option from the Edit menu.

Keyboard conventions

If you're a Windows user new to the Mac, the Return key on the Mac is the same as the Enter key on a PC keyboard, and the Delete key on the Mac is the same as the Backspace key on a PC.

If you're supposed to press several keys at the same time, I indicate that by placing plus signs (+) between them. Thus, Control+⌘+A means press and hold the Control key and the Command key, and then press the A key. After you press the A key, let go of all three keys.

I use the hyphen (–) to join keys to mouse and touchpad move-ments. For example, Option-drag means to hold the Option key while dragging the mouse or your finger.

I provide programming code, full filenames, or filename extensions by formatting such text in a typewriter-like font, `like this`.

Gesture conventions

Because iBooks Author is a Mac application, it doesn't really take advantage of gestures beyond scrolling. But the e-books you produce do respond to gestures when on the iPad, so here's a quick rundown of the gestures your readers are likely to use (and that you should use when testing your e-book in iBooks on an iPad):

- ✔ **Tap:** The most common iPad gesture. It's commonly used to select an item or press a virtual button. To perform a tap, hold your finger over the iPad screen and then quickly touch the screen and lift your finger back up. In other words, tap it.

- ✔ **Double-tap:** Two quick taps in succession. In iBooks, it can act like a contextual mouse click (a right-click) on the Mac or PC, displaying a contextual menu of options for the text you tap. This gesture also can launch a media object and advance slides in a slideshow.

- ✔ **Swipe:** The most common gesture to quickly move through the contents within a window or pane. To swipe on the iPad, place your finger against the screen and drag it for a second or two up and down, or right and left, as the context requires. For example, in iBooks, you can swipe to the left or right to move to the previous or next page, respectively.

- ✔ **Scroll:** The most common gesture to move through items on the screen, such as web pages and lists. iPad apps can use two kinds of scrolling gestures: dragging one or two fingers. Often, dragging two fingers scrolls within a pane or other fixed area, whereas dragging one finger drags the entire screen's contents. Unlike swiping, scrolling moves the contents as far as you drag your fingers proportionally to the screen's dimensions. In iBooks, a one-finger scroll is used to move from one page to another: Scroll to the left to go to the previous page; scroll to the right to go to the next page. If you scroll a page by using two fingers, you get the same effect as pinching a page. When scrolling, lift your finger off the screen when done. A swipe scrolls through one page's worth of contents in iBooks.

- ✔ **Pinch:** Many apps use the pinch gesture to zoom in. iBooks also uses the gesture to shrink a page and move it back to the book's bar of page previews (in landscape orientation) or open the book's table of contents (in portrait orientation). You can also use the pinch gesture to shrink a slideshow back to its container. To perform a pinch, place your thumb and index finger on the screen at the same time and then pinch them together.

✔ **Expand:** The opposite gesture of pinch is expand, which is used to zoom out, such as to make a slideshow expand from its container to the full screen. Put both your index finger and thumb on the screen close to each other, then move them away from each other.

✔ **Rotate:** Use the rotate gesture to rotate objects on the screen, such as 3D objects in iBooks. To do so, place your thumb and index finger on the screen as if starting the pinch gesture, but instead of pinching, rotate your fingers on the screen clockwise or counterclockwise.

Mac interface terms

Finally, let me explain some Mac OS X interface terms you probably don't know the names of but use every day:

✔ **Button:** An area, usually indicated via an outline around it, that you click to make the Mac do the button's function.

✔ **Icon button:** A button indicated via a graphical icon rather than by a word or phrase.

✔ **Menu:** A list of options for the current application that comes from the row of options at the very top of the screen. (The various types of menus are explained in the "Menu commands" section, earlier in this introduction.)

✔ **Pop-up menu:** A menu usually inside a dialog box, panel, bar, or other object, often indicated with either a down-pointing triangle to its right or a pair of triangles to its right.

✔ **Icon menu:** A menu indicated via a graphical icon, rather than by a word or phrase.

✔ **Contextual menu:** A menu of options for an object that appears when you right-click or Control-click that object.

✔ **Field:** A space in which you enter text to provide a value, such as the angle of rotation in the Rotation field.

✔ **Stepper controls:** A pair of triangles, usually one pointing up and one pointing down. When you click the triangles, the adjacent field's values either decrease or increase, depending on which triangle you click.

✔ **Dialog box:** A movable container for user controls — pop-up menus, stepper controls, fields, buttons, and so on — that when open doesn't let you use other controls in the application. You usually have to click OK or Done to apply the settings and close the dialog box.

✔ **Panel:** A movable container for user controls that remains open and available for use; you can use other parts of the application when it's open.

✔ **Pane:** A division within a dialog box, window, or panel. Often, you move from one pane to the other by clicking a tab or label with its name. In some cases, the panes are adjacent to each other, such as in a French door's window panes.

✔ **Settings sheet:** A container for controls that appears at the top of a window or dialog box. Like a dialog box, it prevents you from using other controls until you close the settings sheet. Unlike a dialog box, you can't change its position.

✔ **Bar:** A fixed area of the application window that contains controls, often icon buttons. The most common bar is the toolbar that appears at the top of many application windows. Some bars can be hidden when not in use.

✔ **Title bar:** The top area of a window, dialog box, or panel that indicates its name or its contents' name.

✔ **Close box:** The leftmost circular button in the title bar of a window or panel; clicking it closes the window or panel.

Icons in This Book

This icon highlights an important point that you don't want to forget because it just might come up again. Definitely pay attention to these details.

When this book discusses some really technical details, this icon warns you. Read the text that this icon points to only if you want to get some non-essential information, or you can just skip ahead if you don't want the gory details.

Pay special attention to the paragraphs that feature this icon because they offer you useful tidbits and helpful solutions.

Look out! This icon tells you how to avoid trouble before it starts. Be sure to read and follow the accompanying information.

Where to Go from Here

All right, enough introduction. It's time to get into iBooks Author itself. Because iBooks Author is a new program and works differently than other programs you may be familiar with, such as word processors and page layout software, it's best to read the book's chapters in order so that you can build on the key concepts while you go along.

If you're impatient and experienced in other applications, you can skip or skim Chapter 1 and dive into Chapter 2, which lays out the fundamental concepts in iBooks Author that affect how you create the e-book itself and work within iBooks Author. And if you're an experienced user of Apple Pages, most of Chapter 3 will be familiar to you because iBooks Author uses the same techniques for editing text as Pages does; so you can just skim that chapter.

Some of the iBooks Author concepts — such as its different treatment of portrait and landscape orientations — really do bring you into new territory, so don't rush it. Read this book on your iPad, Kindle, or other device, and have iBooks Author running on your Mac so that you can actually try out the techniques and features this book describes. You can go from theory to practice that much faster.

Chapter 1

What iBooks Author Can Do for You

In This Chapter

▶ Comparing types of e-books

▶ Understanding what sets iBooks Author apart

*R*eading books on an iPad or other electronic device is a wonderful thing. You can carry as many books as you want without increasing the weight. You can search the book, add annotations, and have it available no matter what device you've picked up (thanks to the automatic syncing in most e-readers). But the typical e-book is limited in what it can display: basic text and simple images. That simplicity allows e-books to work on all sorts of devices, but at a price of limited user experience.

iBooks Author brings visual richness to e-books — well, e-books read on an iPad, anyhow. And that richness goes far beyond allowing a more print-like layout; iBooks Author supports a wide range of dynamic content that can make an e-book feel as much like an app as a book. That rich approach has amazing potential for book authors to exploit in ways that the standard e-book simply doesn't.

Comparing iBooks Author to Standard E-Books

E-books — books distributed electronically for reading on a computer, tablet, e-reader, or smartphone — have never been all the same. Amazon.com's Kindle e-readers use their own format (called

Mobi) for such e-books, for example, and even the ePub standard used by the Apple iPad and iPhone, the Barnes & Noble Nook, and other devices varies from device to device in terms of the capabilities it supports. In other words, there's no such thing as a universal e-book, though the basic ePub format comes close.

New to the mix of e-book formats is the format produced by Apple's iBooks Author application for viewing only on Apple's wildly popular iPad tablets. Apple calls this format a Multi-Touch e-book. Like the ePub format used in the standard e-books at the iBookstore, iBooks Author's Multi-Touch format lets you provide text with basic formatting (such as headlines, boldface, and italics), bitmapped graphics (such as photos, screenshots, and converted illustrations), basic tables, and hyperlinks to contents inside the book, as well as on the web.

If this sounds an awful lot like what you can do with the web's HTML (Hypertext Markup Language), it should — the ePub format is in fact a subset of the HTML standard. But unlike creating e-books by using traditional tools such as Adobe InDesign and the open source Sigil, you don't have to understand HTML to rework the e-book files that iBooks Author produces to get what you really intended in your documents. That's a big advantage for iBooks Author over other tools that typically require you to get down and dirty into the HTML code they produce to include anything more than simple text and simple images in your e-book.

Not so for iBooks Author: It directly produces the code for all such elements, and many more that the ePub format can't handle at all. So say good-bye to needing to be an HTML coder to do more than a plain e-book.

Of course, there's a downside to iBooks Author's sophistication: You can't create an ePub e-book from it. That means you can't create e-books for iBooks or other e-readers, iPhones, iPod touches, or other devices — only for iBooks on the iPad. If you want e-books that work on these other devices, you have to create such books with other tools, even if they use the same text and some of the same images.

iBooks Author adds extra capabilities that transform an e-book into a dynamic reader experience. (You can't read an iBooks Author–created e-book in other e-readers because those e-readers support just the standard ePub format, not Apple's dynamic version of it.)

Some of these iBooks Author capabilities are subtle — for example, iBooks Author e-book uses the font you specify, like a PDF can, rather than whatever font the device's e-reader app chooses, like the ePub format on most devices does.

Other capabilities are much richer, letting you create e-books that are much more than standard books. For example, an iBooks Author e-book can create web widgets that provide web-like functionality. It also allows the use of interactive graphics, so a reader can explore a complex image by clicking or tapping labels. It even supports 3D objects that readers can manipulate onscreen. You can embed videos and audio, such as lecture recordings or interviews. You an embed slideshow presentations. And you can add review questions at the end of each chapter, where readers see their score immediately.

As you can see, an iBooks Author e-book is like no other e-book — not even the standard ePub e-books long available for the iPad and Apple's other iOS devices. Sure, the old e-book format works just fine for text-heavy books, such as novels, and even for many text-oriented books embellished with photos and screen images. So, you'll continue to see such ePub e-books produced for the many devices out there that offer book-reading apps.

But thanks to iBooks Author, you'll also see a new class of e-book that represents a major revolution in book publishing: a move away from a static presentation to an interactive one.

 Apple has initially focused iBooks Author on textbook publishing, thus the inclusion of educational features such a chapter review quizzes, but this dynamic format is just as adept for children's books, how-to books, service manuals, and even financial reports. In fact, when you publish an e-book through Apple's iBookstore, you're not limited to putting it in the textbook section — Apple fully expects publishers to create much more than textbooks with it.

Thus, any document that benefits from access to live information via the web or that benefits from video, audio, and interactive exploration is a candidate for iBooks Author.

Creating E-Books Like No Others

In iBooks Author, the simple fact is that you're producing a very different kind of book than a print book or a standard e-book (such as the ePub books available in the iBookstore or the Mobi-format Kindle e-books available from Amazon.com).

If you're going to use iBooks Author, you need to understand *how* an iBooks Author e-book is unlike other books you may have produced — whether print or e-book.

Dynamic interaction capabilities

iBooks Author offers an amazingly rich set of capabilities. In fact, you're working with different kinds of content than what you can in a print book or standard e-book:

- **Text:** Unlike a print book but like an e-book, you can have hyperlinks and cross-references that a reader can tap to jump to the other content immediately. Hyperlinks in iBooks Author work the same way as any e-book. You create a table of contents in a similar way to standard e-books, and you don't necessarily need to have an index because the reader can simply search the e-book. (In fact, none of the e-book tools even let you create indexes.) But iBooks Author makes it much easier to create hyperlinked cross-references to other parts of the book, as well as to figures and glossary entries, than traditional e-book editing tools do. (Chapter 3 explains how to work with text and Chapter 7 explains how to work with hyperlinks, cross-references, tables of contents, and glossaries.)

- **Tables and charts:** Unlike a print book or other e-book, iBooks Author e-books' tables can include calculations such as those used in spreadsheets. That can save you effort in ensuring the accuracy of data in the tables presented to readers. (Readers can't run those calculations, such as with different data, so this capability is interactive only when creating the e-book.) Likewise, you can create all sorts of charts whose data you can edit and whose display you can control in iBooks Author (again, readers can't edit the data on the iPad). (Chapter 5 explains how to work with tables and charts.)

- **Graphics:** In print books and regular e-books, graphics are static, and if you have a gallery of them, you have to use a lot of pages to show them all. A PDF book can have rollover objects and other forms of interactivity, as well as let you produce slideshow-like image galleries. So can iBooks Author — and its tools are easier than those for PDFs. Plus, it lets you use 3D objects that readers can turn to explore them from any angle; not even PDF files can do that. (Chapter 4 explains how to work with static graphics, and Chapter 6 explains how to work with interactive images, 3D images, and image galleries.)

✔ **Video and audio files:** Of course, print books can't play video or audio. Neither can regular e-books (though they can link to such content to be played in the browser or other app). iBooks Author can play these files directly from the e-book, much as a PDF file can. (Chapter 6 explains how to work with video and audio files.)

✔ **Slideshows:** iBooks Author takes the playback concept to a level no one else does: It gives you the ability to play a slide-show (specifically, in Apple's Keynote format). (Chapter 6 explains how to work with slideshows.)

✔ **Web widgets:** Another only-in-iBooks-Author capability, you can include web functionality by using the HTML and JavaScript languages to access web data or create simple apps that run within the e-book. (Chapter 6 explains how to work with web widgets.)

Landscape and portrait views work very differently

The differences between an iBooks Author e-book and other books are more profound than its interactive capabilities. What you can display to readers differs significantly depending on whether they're holding the iPad in the *landscape* (horizontal) or *portrait* (vertical) orientation. (Chapter 2 explains the layout implications in detail.)

The landscape orientation is very much laid out like a traditional print book or PDF, with faithful reproduction of the layout on the iPad. The layout presentation in iBooks Author is a big change from the traditional e-book, which has very little in the way of layout fidelity.

The portrait orientation ignores most of the layout and instead presents the text as a long scroll. Visual elements often aren't vis-ible in portrait orientation, and many of those that are look very different, as thumbnails that must be tapped to have the full ver-sion appear in a temporary window.

Figure 1-1 shows an example iBooks Author e-book in landscape orientation, and Figure 1-2 shows the same e-book in portrait orien-tation so that you can see some of the differences.

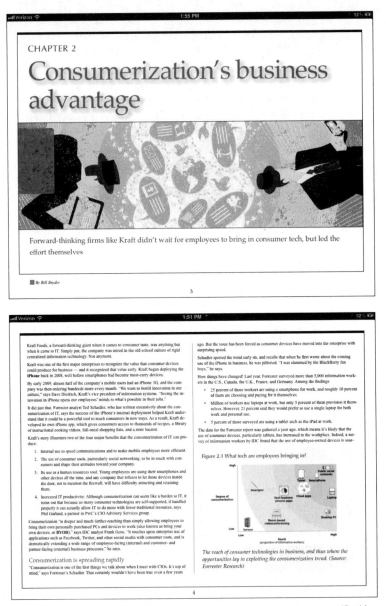

Figure 1-1: Two pages of an iBooks Author e-book layout as seen on an iPad in landscape orientation.

CHAPTER 2
Consumerization's

Forward-thinking firms like Kraft didn't wait for employees to bring in consumer tech, but led the effort themselves

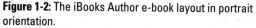

Figure 2.1 What tech are employees bringing in?

Kraft Foods, a forward-thinking giant when it comes to consumer taste, was anything but when it came to IT. Simply put, the company was mired in the old-school culture of rigid centralized information technology. Not anymore.

Kraft was one of the first major enterprises to recognize the value that consumer devices could produce for business — and it recognized that value early. Kraft began deploying the **iPhone** back in 2008, well before smartphones had become must-carry devices.

Figure 1-2: The iBooks Author e-book layout in portrait orientation.

In a nutshell, the portrait orientation of an iBooks Author e-book is more like a traditional e-book, whereas the landscape orientation is more like a traditional print book (or PDF file).

This duality of very different presentation styles can confuse many experienced designers, whether they come from a print or e-book background, so expect your first project to be a learning experience involving much more than the use of a new authoring tool.

Limitations on readers' display controls

Although iBooks Author does many things that no other e-book software can, the e-books it produces lose some capabilities available to regular e-books in the iPad's iBooks app:

✔ Readers can't adjust the size of text for an iBooks Author book when in landscape orientation — the primary orientation for reading e-books created by iBooks Author. And in neither orientation can readers change the font used in an iBooks Author e-book, as they can for a regular e-book.

These two limits mean you need to pay close attention to readability for your intended audience; many designers use text sizes that are way too small for most people over the age of 30. So keep your text to no smaller than 12 points if you want readers to be able to read it. And avoid overly fancy fonts because those are hard to read on screen, especially at small to medium sizes. Ditto with use of light text on dark backgrounds, a popular but hard-to-read effect best kept to small doses of large, bold text — and even worse is designers' current fancy: light text on a white background.

✔ Readers can't change the page color, such as to switch to the night-reading mode of light text on a black background, which is less likely to disturb your sleeping bed partner while you read.

Figure 1-3 shows the controls available for iBooks Author e-books in the iBooks app. The reader taps the screen to display these controls; they disappear after a few seconds if the reader doesn't tap one of them.

The lack of these text-adjustment and page-color controls for iBooks Author books reflects that iBooks Author is designed to create a book much more like a traditional book (or PDF) with a fixed design determined by the layout artist. That design lets iBooks Author do some of the rich presentation unique to it, so the trade-off is well worth it — but avid e-book readers will certainly note the loss of their presentation control.

iBooks library

Bookmark

E-book's TOC   Reader's notes   Screen brightness   Search

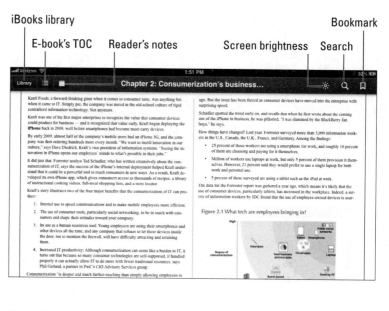

iBooks library

E-book's TOC   Reader's notes   Text size and
                                      screen brightness

Bookmark

Search

Figure 1-3: The controls in iBooks for an iBooks Author e-book, in both landscape orientation (top) and portrait orientation (bottom).

Chapter 2

Putting Together Your Book's Building Blocks

. . . .

In This Chapter

▶ Identifying the elements that make up an iBooks Author e-book

▶ Working with templates, book files, layouts, and objects

▶ Looking at books in portrait and landscape orientations

▶ Creating a book cover

▶ Adding media elements to the intro

▶ Getting a preview of your e-book

. . . .

*O*n the silver screen and in novels, a lonely writer types away at an old Underwood, double-spaced manuscript pages growing in a pile on the desk, with rejected pages balled up in a trash can. Somehow, those manuscript pages become a book. Of course, that's not how it works in the modern world, where (outside of fiction and biographies) books are rarely composed of just text.

Certainly, if all you're doing is creating an all-text book or a mainly-text book with a few photos or diagrams, there's no need to use the layout-savvy, interaction-capable iBooks Author software — instead, just use Apple's Pages word processing program, export the file in the ePub format, and you're done. If you use a different word processor that also offers ePub export, you can use that instead.

But if you're reading this book, your goals are loftier than that. You're intending to produce a book that's rich in one or more ways: graphically presented; layout-savvy; dynamically and interactively illustrated; augmented with videos, presentations, and/or audio (such as for how-to guides, embedded lectures, and from-the-horse's-mouth interviews); and interactively educational (such as with chapter quizzes).

As you can see, an iBooks Author e-book can contain a lot of elements — many, or even most, of which you create outside of iBooks Author and then import. So, you need to think not just about the words or even just the elements, but how they come together for the reader in the final e-book. Web designers and, to a lesser extent, magazine designers are usually familiar with that skill, but not most other people.

Looking at the Containers in Your Book

iBooks Author provides various types of containers to help you bring all the elements of your e-book together. Containers hold one or more elements, and the way you arrange elements within containers, and then containers within the book, determines the reader experience. Some containers are specific to certain types of content, and others hold multiple types of content.

Templates

A template is the most complex container because it contains all the other containers in an arrangement (a *layout*) designed for a specific type of book. iBooks Author comes with several textbook templates that carry the look and feel of common textbooks, similar to the ones you probably used in high school or college. And you can create your own templates. Although their visual styles (such as fonts and use of space) differ, all templates include the same containers.

So, a template is the ultimate container for beginning a book project, the one you choose or create so that you can create the rest of the book based on the template container's elements and structure. (After you save a template for a specific project, you're working in a book file; the bare template remains untouched so that you can create more books by using it in the future.)

Chapters

Books have multiple sections, or *chapters* — usually one chapter for each key topic. Chapters help the reader focus on one specific area at a time, and they can help the author organize the basic content into sensible chunks. (Otherwise, the book would be one overwhelmingly long mass of material.) Chapters are essentially breakpoints within a book.

Layouts

The key building block for pages is the *layout,* which is a visual arrangement and design for the different types of pages you want to have in the book. You can think of a layout as a template for pages. For example, the layout for the opening page of a chapter is likely to be different than the rest of the pages in a chapter, and you likely have special page designs for your foreword, dedication, and so on. You might even have a page variation within a chapter; for example, if your standard chapter layout uses two columns of text, you may also create a six-column layout to use on pages that contain, say, a grid of images with captions.

A layout can contain several designs. iBooks Author offers chapter layouts, section layouts, and page layouts. The relationship of these layouts is hierarchical: A chapter layout applies to all pages in a chapter, a section layout applies to all pages in a section, and a page layout applies to individual pages. If you apply a chapter layout to a chapter, that layout doesn't affect pages that already have a section layout or a page layout, and if you apply a section layout to a section, it doesn't affect pages that already have a page layout applied.

Sections

A section is a division within a chapter — a subchapter, essentially. You don't have to use them, but if your chapters cover several related subtopics, you might have a section for each of those subtopics, with the beginning of the chapter acting as an introduction to the subtopics. You can also use sections for books that have a consistent set of approaches within each chapter, such as a section explaining the concepts, a section showing examples of the concepts applied to real situations, a section of problems to solve, and a section of answers.

The layouts that Apple supplies in its iBooks Author templates include predefined sections for three common needs: forewords, dedications, and copyright pages. You don't have to use them, and of course, you can modify them like you can any layout.

Pages

The first books were produced on scrolls, so you just kept reading until you reached the end of one very long sheet of material. (Well, some books took several scrolls, but you get the idea.) Then, someone invented the notion of the bound book, where people flipped through sheets (pages). That made it easier to store and carry books, and for readers to indicate where they left off (via a slip of paper, or even a reed or twig, inserted between the pages — the original bookmark).

Unlike chapter breaks, page breaks are usually unrelated to any meaning. When a page is full, the material continues onto the next one, whereas a chapter is an intentional break signifying a change in topic. (Although some books may in fact control where content ends on a page, so each page is largely self-contained, in sort of a subchapter approach.)

Although the iPad doesn't use paper, when you're viewing an e-book in *landscape* (horizontal) orientation, it keeps the notion of pages by dividing content based on what fits on the screen: A screen is the electronic version of a paper page, and you flip from one to the next as if reading a bound book.

But when you're viewing an e-book in *portrait* (vertical) orientation, iBooks Author treats pages more like traditional scrolls, where you keep scrolling until the e-book has ended — there's just one long page.

This duality means a page in an iBooks Author book has two versions — the portrait version and the landscape version — to accommodate the iPad's ability to rotate its screen and its contents accordingly. That rotation means that the number of pages and where text breaks across pages can differ simply based on how the reader is holding the iPad. The design of the pages in the two orientations also differs dramatically, as I explain in the section "Portrait versus Landscape Orientation," later in this chapter.

Objects

The building blocks of your book are objects, which hold specific content such as text, captions, photos, slideshows, web snippets, diagrams, and so on. iBooks Author categorizes these objects into five groups: text boxes, shapes, tables, charts, and widgets. (Widgets contain the interactive elements, such as slideshows, web snippets, videos, 3D graphics, and quizzes.)

How these objects appear to the reader varies based on the orientation in which she's viewing the e-book:

✔ **Landscape orientation:** Your basic chapter text — called a *mainbar* by traditional book and magazine designers — flows from page to page in an automatically created frame provided by the layout applied to the pages.

When you're in landscape orientation, the other objects in an iBooks Author e-book appear where you insert them, like in a traditional paper book layout. You can insert them as *floating objects,* meaning they stay put while the text reflows around them, or you can insert them as *anchored objects,* which means their location is tied to specific text, so the objects move with the text. (I explain the two types of objects in the section "Understanding inline, anchored, and floating objects," later in this chapter.)

✔ **Portrait orientation:** The mainbar text flows continuously within a section's single scrolling page.

In portrait orientation, widgets typically shrink into icons in the open left margin (called a *rail* by publishers and the *thumbnail track* by iBooks Author), and readers can click those icons to open the full window of whatever the widget contains. Objects at the beginning of chapters and sections remain in the mainbar — they're not iconized or moved to the thumbnail track. Floating objects that don't have titles and captions in the rest of a chapter or section don't appear in portrait orientation (see Chapter 5). Inline objects (explained in the section "Understanding inline, anchored, and floating objects," later in this chapter) *are* displayed when the e-book is in portrait orientation.

In both landscape and portrait orientations, each chapter or section may have special objects, such as a title and images, that precede the mainbar text to let you know that you're in a new chapter or section.

Styles

A critical building block in any book is its set of styles (known as a *style sheet* by print designers and contained in the *style drawer* in iBooks Author), which control text formatting, from its font to whether it's hyphenated, from the spacing between lines and paragraphs to its margin alignment. By using styles, you define these attributes just once and then apply them consistently to all text, instead of having to remember all the settings and applying them individually. Plus, if you change a style's definition, all text that uses the style is automatically updated to have the new definition — a huge time-saver.

There are two types of styles: paragraph styles, which affect the entire paragraph, and character styles, which affect only the specific text to which you apply them. All text has a paragraph style applied to it, but the use of character styles is optional, for when you want to make specific text different from the rest of the paragraph.

For example, say you want to highlight the first few words of a bulleted list in blue bold Arial text but display the rest of the paragraph in black normal Times text. In this situation, you set the paragraph style to black normal Times and the character style to blue bold Arial, and then you highlight the introductory text for each bullet and apply the character style to it. Chapter 3 explains how to work with styles.

You can also create a text box style in iBooks Author, which lets you set attributes such as background color, encasing line, and spacing for sidebars and other text boxes that you use in your book. Chapters 3 and 5 explain how to work with text boxes.

Opening and Saving Templates and Book Files

To create a new iBooks Author project, you must start by selecting a template, which you do by choosing File⇨New or pressing ⌘+N to open the Template Chooser shown in Figure 2-1. If you want to see larger or smaller thumbnails of the templates, drag the slider at the bottom of the screen. Select the desired template and click Choose to create a book file from it.

Figure 2-1: The Template Chooser.

Working with document versions

Keep in mind that Mac OS X Lion has changed how applications save files. Documents in Lion-savvy applications such as iBooks Author automatically save changes when you make them. Also, there's no File➪Save As menu option that you may be used to in Windows and previous versions of Mac OS X. You can choose File➪Duplicate to save a copy of the file with a different name.

Like with earlier versions of Mac OS X and with Windows, when you first save a document by choosing File➪Save, you have to give the file a name and select a location, but after that point, choosing File➪Save (or pressing ⌘+S) saves the updated file. But in Lion-savvy applications such as iBooks Author, choosing File➪Save (or pressing ⌘+S) after the first time saves a version of the document within the same file. You can go back to those earlier by choosing File➪Revert Document.

Also new to Mac OS X Lion is automatic file locking after a file has been unopened for a period set in the Time Machine system preference's Options settings sheet. If a file is locked, Locked appears to the right of its name in the document's title bar; click the adjacent triangle icon to unlock the file, or unlock the file when prompted to do so when you save a version.

If you use the same template over and over again, you can tell iBooks Author to always use that template when creating a new project. Just follow these steps:

1. **Choose iBooks Author➪Preferences.**

   Alternatively, you can press ⌘+, (comma).

   The General Preferences dialog box opens.

2. **Select the Use Template option in the General pane.**

   A settings sheet opens, displaying a miniature version of the Template Chooser.

3. **Click the icon of the desired template to select it.**

4. **Click Choose to choose the template, and then close the General Preferences dialog box.**

To change the template used, reopen the General Preferences dialog box and select a different template. To stop iBooks Author from using a specific template automatically for new documents, select Show Template Chooser, rather than Use Template.

If you have iBooks Author set to use a template automatically for new documents, you can still select a new template by choosing File⇨New from Template Chooser or pressing Shift+⌘+N (rather than the usual File⇨New or ⌘+N).

If you want to use an existing book, rather than a template, as the basis for your new book, you have several options:

✔ In the Template Chooser, choose a recent file from the Open Recent pop-up menu.

✔ In the Template Chooser, click the Open Existing File button, and in the Open dialog box that appears, navigate to the desired file, select it, and click Open.

✔ From the menu bar, choose File⇨Open (or press ⌘+O), and then in the Open dialog box that appears, navigate to the desired file, select it, and click Open.

If you use an existing book as your template, you need to remove the contents from that book after you save the new book with a different name or to a different location. To create that copy of the book, choose File⇨Duplicate. Otherwise, you lose that original book's contents and layout when you adjust the opened file.

I strongly suggest that as soon as you create a new project from a template and know you want to use it for your book, you save it as a book file by following these steps:

1. **Choose File⇨Save.**

   Alternatively, you can press ⌘+S.

2. **(Optional) In the Save settings sheet that appears, type a new filename in the Save As field and select a new location in the settings sheet, as Figure 2-2 shows.**

   If you don't see the settings sheet shown in Figure 2-2, click the down-pointing triangle button to the right of the Save As field.

3. **Click the Save button.**

By immediately saving your project file after creating it from a template, you're less likely to have to redo work if your Mac loses power. Although iBooks Author automatically saves files while you work on them, you need to create the specific file that you want to save, and that book file is created only after you first save the document created from a template.

To save a book as a template for reuse later, choose File⇨Save as Template. Before you save an existing book as a template, you might want to remove any elements from the book that you don't want to use as examples or standards in the template so that you don't unnecessarily clutter that template.

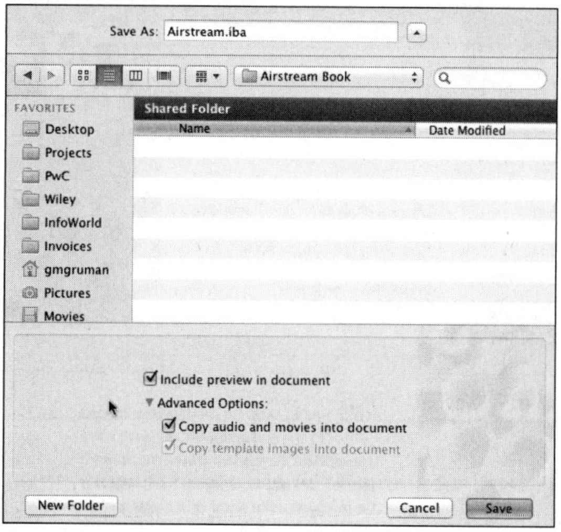

Figure 2-2: The full Save As settings sheet.

Working with Layouts

After you create a book from a template or open an existing book, and then save it in the appropriate location for your project, you can start working on the book. Figure 2-3 shows what a new book created from a template looks like.

Chances are that you first want to make some basic modifications to the template if this is the first book you're creating by using it. That means modifying the various layouts in the book, as well as the styles. (Chapter 3 covers creating, modifying, and using styles.) By default, you see the Book panel at the left side of the screen. At top, it contains the borderless buttons that you can click to open the views for working on your book's title, any media file (video or audio) you want to play when a book is first opened, your book's table of contents, and your book's glossary. (Chapter 7 explains these capabilities.) Below those four buttons are any chapters in your book and any sections in those chapters, including all the pages that exist.

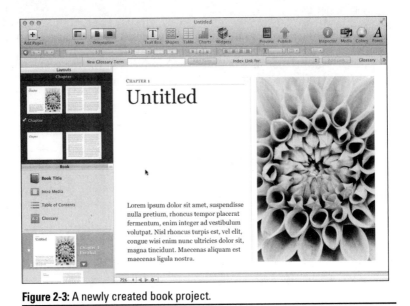

Figure 2-3: A newly created book project.

Layouts differ depending on whether you're working on landscape or portrait orientation, which I explain in depth in the section "Portrait versus Landscape Orientation," later in this chapter. A chapter's or section's landscape layout has two pages: The left page applies to the first page in that chapter or section, and the right page applies to all subsequent pages in that chapter or section. By contrast, a portrait layout has just one long page that applies to the entire chapter or section.

If you prefer to see an outline-style list of your pages, rather than thumbnails, in the Book panel, choose View➪Book Outline. To see thumbnails, choose View➪Page Thumbnails. You can also use the View icon button in the toolbar to switch between these views.

The objects used in layouts can be regular objects or placeholders. Any object you put in the layout is used as-is on all pages based on that layout. That's great for elements that you want on all such pages, such as a square containing the page number or a ruling line that divides columns. But it's not so great for objects that you want to customize, such as the photo in a chapter opener or the placeholder text in the mainbar and other text boxes. That's why iBooks Author lets you specify whether you want to be able to modify a layout object's contents on pages. (I explain in the section "Specifying placeholders," later in this chapter, how to specify that permission on each object.)

Layout view controls

To work on layouts, you use the Layouts panel, shown in Figure 2-3, to select the layout you want to modify. (iBooks Author's templates come with several predefined layouts.) That panel doesn't appear by default, so choose View⇨Layouts to open it. (Choose View⇨Layouts again to hide it.)

To create a new layout, rather than edit an existing one, select an existing layout in the Layouts panel, choose Insert⇨Layouts, and then choose the desired layout type from the submenu that appears. (You can also click the Add Layout button in the toolbar.) iBooks Author inserts a new layout that's a copy of the selected one.

Not all objects are fully visible in a layout; the boundaries (frames) of text boxes, for example, may not be obvious, even if they contain placeholder text, because of the margins assigned to the text boxes. And by default, the boundaries appear only if you select a text box or other object. To force the boundaries to display regardless of whether objects are selected, choose View⇨Show Layout Boundaries (or press Shift+⌘+L). (Hide the boundaries by choosing View⇨Hide Layout Boundaries or pressing Shift+⌘+L.) You can see these boundaries — simply a rectangle indicating the object frame — in Figure 2-4's sample layout.

Another handy control for viewing layouts and pages — especially on smaller screens, such as on a MacBook Air — is the Zoom menu. Choose View⇨Zoom, and then choose one of the submenu options:

- Zoom In (or, rather than use the menu, press Shift+⌘+. [period])
- Zoom Out (or press Shift+⌘+, [comma])
- Actual Size
- Fit Width
- Fit Page

Fit Width makes sure the full layout width is visible onscreen, but some of the page depth could be cut off and require scrolling to see; Fit Page shows the entire layout.

Creating a shortcut for the Fit Page view

Unfortunately, each time you switch to a different layout, iBooks Author resets the view to Actual Size, instead of remembering your last setting, so on a small screen, you may find yourself using the Fit Page zoom option a lot — and wish it had a keyboard shortcut. Fortunately, Mac OS X Lion lets you create your own shortcuts. Just follow these steps:

1. **In the Keyboard system preference's Keyboard Shortcuts pane, select the Applications Shortcut option in the left pane, and then click the + (plus sign) icon button.**

   A settings sheet appears with the Application pop-up menu, the Menu Title field, and the Keyboard Shortcut field.

   If you're new to Mac OS X, you go to a system preference by choosing ⌘⇨System Preferences to open the System Preferences application, and then click the icon for the specific system preference you want to open.

2. **In the Application pop-up menu, choose iBooks Author.**

3. **In the Menu Title field, enter Fit Page.**

4. **In the Keyboard Shortcut field, enter your desired shortcut.**

   I use Option+Shift+⌘+0 because I do so consistently in other programs I use regularly.

5. **Click Add to save the shortcut and close the settings sheet.**

6. **Close the Systems Preferences application.**

   When you return to working in iBooks Author, it now has that new shortcut available.

Layouts versus pages

Layouts are essentially templates for pages, so the means to create, edit, and adjust the objects and settings for layouts are the same as for pages (covered in the section "Applying and modifying layouts," later in this chapter). The difference is that if you modify a layout, it affects all future pages based on it (as well as pages you explicitly reapply it to), whereas if you modify a page, only that page is modified.

Another key difference between layouts and pages is the intent. The objects in your layouts should be ones you plan to use repeatedly in your e-book. For example, you may want an object for the chapter title and page number to appear on all pages, so you put these objects in your template. And you may always plan to have an image on your chapter's opening page, in which case, you put a placeholder image on your chapter template's first page.

But you may not have tables, videos, and the like in a predefined position throughout your book, so they're probably not appropriate to place in a template, but should be placed when needed in actual book pages. Of course, you may want to standardize some formatting, such as making sure certain common elements — tables or web widgets, for example — always have a certain width or a certain format. In these cases, it may make sense to create a page layout that contains such standardized placeholders; even if the position on the page varies, having such page layouts gives you an easily accessible library from which you can copy such objects, even if you don't actually base any book pages on those page layouts. (There's no law that says you have to apply every layout you have to actual pages, after all.)

Applying and modifying layouts

When you complete your layouts, you apply them to your book either by adding pages based on them or applying them to existing pages. You can also modify your layouts for use in new pages or to update existing pages. (I cover how to work with the actual objects in a layout in the following section because they apply to both layouts and book pages.)

Applying a different layout to an existing page is easy. Select the page in the Book panel. The down-pointing triangle button that appears is a universal indicator in Mac OS X for a pop-up menu. Click the triangle to display a pop-up menu of available layouts (as Figure 2-4 shows), choose the desired layout from the menu of thumbnails that appears, and watch the page's layout change accordingly. You can also right-click or Control-click a page, and then choose Change Page Layout from the contextual menu that appears; in fact, you must use this method when in portrait view.

You use the same process for chapters and sections. If you select a chapter, you get just chapter layouts; if you select a section, you get just section layouts; and if you select a page, you get just page layouts.

You can control the display of items in the Book panel. The first pages in a chapter are aligned to the left, section pages are indented slightly, and non-layout-based pages are indented even further. Note the small gray triangle (called a *disclosure triangle*) to the left of the first page in a chapter or section:

✔ **If the disclosure triangle is pointing down:** All the chapter's or section's pages appear below it.

✔ **If the disclosure triangle is pointing to the right:** The pages are hidden from view in the Book panel.

Click the disclosure triangle to toggle between the two views.

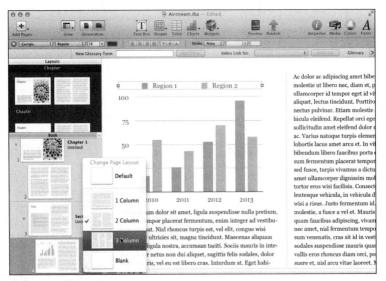

Figure 2-4: You can apply a new layout to a selected page via the Book panel.

As Figure 2-5 shows, you may see an additional option in the menu of layouts: Reapply Layout to Chapter, Reapply Layout to Section, or Reapply Layout to Page, depending on what you've selected. That option appears if the layout has been changed since it was first applied to that chapter, section, or page.

But you don't have to select each chapter, section, or page one by one and reapply a changed layout to each. When you change a template, the red Apply Changes button appears below the template's preview in the Layouts panel when in landscape orientation and to the right of the template's name when in portrait orientation. Click the button to update all pages based on that layout.

When you apply a different layout to a chapter, section, or page — or when you apply an updated layout to it — any local changes in your book are preserved. For example, if your updated chapter layout moves the text box containing the chapter title, all chapters based on that layout have the corresponding chapter title text boxes moved, but any text changes and added objects remain untouched. Similarly, if you change a page from a two-column layout to a three-column layout, as shown in Figure 2-4, any floating objects added to the page (such as the chart) are left as-is; the text continues to flow around those objects. (Inline objects and anchored objects may move, as explained in the section "Understanding inline, anchored, and floating objects," later in this chapter.)

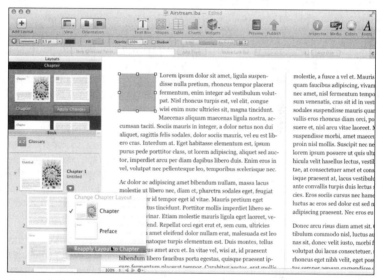

Figure 2-5: Apply an updated layout to a selected chapter via the Book panel.

The Basics of Page and Layout Objects

After you create a book from a template (as described in the preceding sections), you probably want to actually create the book's contents. The new book you're working with already has elements in it, in its layouts and perhaps in pages. But you have more to add, and you probably want to modify the layouts provided by the template to your design taste. Chapter 4 gets into the details of working with objects, such as formatting them, positioning them, sizing them, and adjusting their attributes. The following sections explain the basics so that you can begin experimenting with the various layout and page containers.

Adding chapters, sections, and pages

The three basic content containers in an iBooks Author e-book — chapters, sections, and pages — share many of the techniques when it comes to adding them to your book. But there are some differences you should know.

Adding chapters

To add chapters to a book, you have four options:

- ✔ Drag the chapter layout from the Layouts panel into the Book panel. When you release the mouse button or touch-pad pointer, iBooks Author adds a new chapter by using that layout after the chapter onto which you dropped the layout (after you released the mouse button, of course).

- ✔ If the Book panel is active, click the Add Pages icon button in the toolbar. A menu of layout types that you can apply to the added page appears: chapter, section, or page. Each, in turn, has a thumbnail list of existing layouts. Choose the desired layout type and then the desired layout, and a chapter, section, or page based on that layout is inserted after the last page in the current chapter or section.

- ✔ In the Book panel, right-click or Control-click a chapter, then choose Duplicate Chapter from the contextual menu to copy that chapter (including its contents) after the current chapter. You can also choose Copy Chapter, then go elsewhere in the Book panel, right-click or Control-click again, and choose Paste from the contextual menu that appears to insert the chapter after that location.

- ✔ Create a new chapter by inserting a Word or Pages document (choose Insert⇨Chapter from Pages or Word Document). A settings sheet where you can choose the document appears, and after you select a document and click Insert, a second settings sheet showing the available layouts appears. (You can also select the Preserve Document Paragraph Styles on Import check box, which loads the paragraph and character styles defined in that document.) Pick the layout you want to apply, and then click Choose. (Chapter 3 covers this method in detail.)

Adding sections

To add sections to a book, you can use the first three methods in the preceding section (the drag method, the Add Pages icon button, and the contextual menu), except you work with a section rather than a chapter.

Adding pages

To add pages to a book, you can use the first two methods in the section "Adding chapters," earlier in this chapter (the drag method and the Add Pages icon button), working with pages rather than chapters. But you also have two other methods available:

- ✔ Right-click or Control-click any page (chapter, section, or page) in the Book panel, then choose Insert Page from the contextual menu that appears. A new page, which uses the selected page's layout template, is added below that page.

- ✔ Right-click or Control-click a chapter page in the Book panel, then choose Add Page from the contextual menu that appears. A new page, which uses the chapter layout's right-page template, is added before the start of the following section.

 You can add only one page at a time (except when you're importing a Word or Pages file). Likewise, you can delete only one page at a time (right-click or Control-click the page, and then choose Delete Page from the contextual menu that appears).

Navigating pages and layouts

To go to a page, double-click it in the Book panel (or, for a layout, in the Layout panel). To maneuver through your pages, first select the chapter or section whose pages you want to scroll through in the Book panel. Then, you can use any of three methods to go through your pages:

- ✔ Scroll sideways by clicking the scrollbars, scrolling with the mouse's scroll wheel or touch surface (if it has either), or using the touchpad's sideways scrolling gesture. *Note:* You can't scroll across chapters or sections this way, just within them.

- ✔ Press the keyboard's up-arrow and down-arrow keys to move from page to page within the current chapter or section. Press ⌘+up arrow to go to the first page in that chapter or section, and ⌘+down arrow to go to the last page in that chapter or section. *Note:* You can't scroll across chapters or sections this way, just within them.

- ✔ Click the two triangle icon buttons at the bottom of the iBooks Author application window. Click the up-pointing-triangle icon button to scroll back (in landscape orientation) or up (in portrait orientation); click the down-pointing-triangle icon button to scroll forward (or down). Open the Actions icon menu (which looks like a gear) and choose the desired scrolling behavior as shown in Figure 2-6: from page to page, section to section, chapter to chapter, figure label to figure label, glossary term to glossary term, bookmark to bookmark, use of a specified paragraph style to the next use, or use of a specified character style to the next use.

Figure 2-6: You use the Actions icon menu to choose the scrolling behavior in iBooks Author.

Adding objects to layouts and pages

iBooks Author supports a wide variety of objects:

✔ **Text boxes:** These objects contain text. iBooks Author has predefined mainbar text boxes that let the book's main text flow from page to page, but you can create additional text boxes, such as for sidebars, intro lists, and the like. (Chapter 3 explains how to create, edit, and format text, and Chapter 5 explains how to format the boxes themselves.)

✔ **Images:** You can import a variety of image files, including GIF, Illustrator (`.ai`), JPEG, PDF, Photoshop (`.psd`), PICT, PNG, RAW, TIFF, and Windows Bitmap (`.bmp`).

If you import a multipage PDF file, only the first page appears in the book. Also, older Illustrator files may not import, and Illustrator EPS files definitely don't import.

✔ **Shapes:** iBooks Author has 15 predefined shapes, as well as a Bézier pen tool that you can use to draw your own shapes. (Chapter 5 explains how to work with these shapes.)

✔ **Tables:** Tables not only contain text, but also can contain live formulas. (Chapter 5 explains how to work with tables.)

✔ **Charts:** You can create 19 types of charts and edit their data. (Chapter 5 explains how to work with charts.)

✔ **Widgets:** iBooks Author supports seven types of interactive widgets: galleries (of images), media (audio and video), reviews (multiple-choice quizzes), Apple Keynote slideshows, interactive images (with callouts that expand when tapped), 3D images, and web snippets. (Chapter 6 explains how to work with widgets.)

These objects can all be added to a layout or page, be positioned and sized as desired, and have attributes such as fill and borders adjusted. All can be made into anchored objects, and some can be used as inline objects, as I explain in the following section.

Chapter 4 explains the details of adding the contents to such objects, but here's a summary so that you can experiment with them while working on layouts and basic pages:

✔ Drag a supported file from the Finder into an iBooks Author layout or page. (If the file is supported, a green circle that contains a white + [plus sign] appears when the pointer is in the iBooks Author window.) An object is created where you release the pointer. In the case of text-only (.txt) and Rich Text Format (.rtf) files, the text is inserted into an existing text box if you drop the file into existing text, or it's placed into a separate text box if dropped elsewhere in the layout. And graphics are anchored to the text you drag and drop them in; if you drop the graphics outside a text box, they're placed as *floating* (independent) objects.

✔ Choose Insert⇨Choose or press Shift+⌘+V to open a settings sheet in which you navigate the Mac's contents for any type of compatible file. (Compatible files are displayed in black, incompatible files appear in gray.) You can't insert text formats, such as .txt and .rtf, via this menu or shortcut, but you can drag and drop them into an iBooks Author file.

✔ Choose Insert from the menu bar and then the desired type of object from the menu to insert it as a floating object. For example, you might choose Insert⇨Table to insert a table.

✔ In the toolbar, click the Text Box or Table icon button, or use the Shapes, Charts, or Widgets icon menus, to insert the chosen object as a floating object.

Understanding inline, anchored, and floating objects

Most objects in iBooks Author can have any of three states — floating, anchored, and inline:

✔ **Floating object:** In landscape orientation, it stays on the page where it's placed and in the location on that page, regardless of how the text flows. In portrait orientation, it appears in the thumbnail track at the page's left if it has a caption applied, as Chapter 5 explains.

✔ **Anchored object:** In landscape orientation, it moves from page to page with the specific text it's associated with (anchored to); it moves pages only if its anchor text moves pages, and its position on the new page is the same as on the old one. In portrait orientation, it appears in the thumbnail track at the page's left if it has a caption applied.

✔ **Inline object:** In both orientations, it moves in step with its text anchor; for example, if the anchor moves two lines down, so does the object.

Widgets can't be inserted as inline objects, just as floating and anchored objects.

Introducing the Inspector

If you use any of Apple's iWork applications — Pages, Numbers, or Keynote — you know the Inspector panel. It's also a fundamental element when working in iBooks Author. The Inspector has nine panes of options for a selected object, letting you modify all sorts of settings. Figure 2-7 shows several of them.

Some options apply to the entire document, but most are just for the selected object. Thus, the capabilities in each pane change based on what object is selected. They can also differ based on whether you're working on a layout or a page. Some capabilities that don't apply to the current context simply don't appear, and others appear but are grayed out, so you can't access them. If no object is selected, the Inspector can still be opened, but it lets you control only settings related to the entire book document.

To display (or hide) the Inspector, click the Inspector icon button in the toolbar, choose View⇨Show Inspector (or Hide Inspector), or press Option+⌘+I. You can also close the Inspector by clicking the Close button in its title bar.

Although they are simply panes in the Inspector panel, Apple's documentation refers to each inspector as if it were a separate panel, such as the Layout inspector and the Document inspector. This book uses the Apple terminology (and thus also calls the various Inspector panes' subpanes simply panes). I use *Inspector* to mean the panel and *inspector* (such as Layout inspector) when referring to a specific pane.

You can have more than one inspector visible by choosing View⇨New Inspector. All open inspectors apply to the selected object, providing a handy way to see several panes at the same time, rather than switch among them.

To go to a specific inspector, you open the Inspector panel and then click its corresponding icon button at the top. The title bar changes to the name of that particular inspector.

Here's what the various inspectors do:

- ✔ **Document:** Go to the Document pane to open document information such as word counts and set metadata such as author name (see Chapter 7), turn off portrait orientation, turn on hyphenation and ligatures (see Chapter 3), and specify whether you want to require a password for someone to open the book document. The TOC pane lets you specify which paragraph styles are used to determine what appears in the table of contents (see Chapter 7).

- ✔ **Layout:** Its Layout pane lets you set the number of columns in a selected text box, and the Numbering pane lets you set section and page numbering for the current page (regardless of whether an object is selected). Chapter 7 explains section and page numbering.

- ✔ **Wrap:** This inspector lets you control whether an object is floating, anchored, or inline, as well as whether and how text wraps around the object. Chapter 4 covers wrap formatting.

- ✔ **Text:** The four panes let you control text formatting for the selected paragraph, such as line spacing and indentation, bullets and numbering, tab positions, borders and backgrounds, language, how lines within a paragraph can break across columns and pages, document-wide hyphenation controls, and what paragraph style is applied to the following paragraph. In the More pane, you can also adjust the text position up or down for selected text. Chapter 3 covers text formatting.

- ✔ **Graphic:** This inspector lets you apply a fill, stroke (outline), and drop shadow to images, charts, and widgets, as well as transparency (opacity) to images and charts. You can also apply strokes to table cells. Chapter 5 covers graphics formatting.

- ✔ **Metric:** This inspector lets you specify the size and position of objects, as well as their rotation and whether they're flipped. For images, it also lets you constrain the proportions to prevent resized images from being distorted, as well as resize an image to its original size, as Chapter 4 explains.

- ✔ **Table:** Its Table pane lets you set the parameters for a table, including number of rows and columns, borders, colors, and cell sizes. It also provides controls for sorting, deleting, inserting, and splitting rows and columns, as well as setting headers and footers. The Format pane lets you determine formatting for individual cells, such as number display, and apply live calculations and rules to the contents of cells for dynamic tables. Chapter 5 covers the creation and formatting of tables.

✔ **Chart:** This inspector lets you determine the chart's visual style, edit its data, and specify how its elements (such as captions and axes) appear, as Chapter 5 details.

✔ **Link:** The Hyperlink pane lets you create hyperlinks to web pages and items within the e-book, and the Bookmarks pane lets you add destination anchors (bookmarks) in the document so that you can create hyperlinks to them. Chapter 7 explains these capabilities.

✔ **Widget:** The Layout pane lets you set how the caption and title appear on widgets such as movies, and you can also set a background and margin for the contents. The Interaction pane lets you specify whether to force a widget to run in full-screen mode when a reader taps it. Chapter 6 covers widgets.

Figure 2-7: Four iBooks Author inspectors.

Specifying placeholders

In a layout (versus in a book page), you often want to have placeholder objects that are replaced with specific content in the e-book's actual pages.

When you insert a widget in a layout by using the corresponding menu or toolbar icon menu or icon button (described in the section "Adding objects to layouts and pages," earlier in this chapter), the item is by default a placeholder. (You see a gray placeholder icon, such as a movie filmstrip, indicating that the object is a placeholder.)

The same is true for a table, image, text box, or chart that has a caption applied to it (see Chapter 5). And the mainbar text boxes in a template are also placeholders, meaning their text is editable on the actual book pages.

But other objects (such as a shape, photo, text box, or other object that doesn't have a caption applied to it) are treated as parts of the template to be repeated as-is on each page that uses the layout. But you can convert such objects to placeholders and make their contents editable on book pages. To do so, select the object, and then open the Layout inspector. In its Layout pane, select the Editable on Pages Using This Layout check box.

For text, you can edit the placeholder text, if desired. The iBooks Author templates use fake Latin text for the mainbar placeholders, so its formatting appears on book pages created from that template's layout until you substitute the actual text. Text boxes you create yourself have the placeholder text Type to Enter Text.

You can change this text and its formatting, as desired. Then you can lock that placeholder text and its formatting in the layout so that it appears consistently on all pages created from it: Choose Format⇨Advanced⇨Disable Placeholder Text Editing. (To edit or format that placeholder text in your layout, choose Format⇨Advanced⇨Enable Placeholder Text Editing.)

Sometimes, you may have a text box that contains a mix of fixed text and placeholder text. In the layout, select the text in such a text box that you do *not* want to be a placeholder, and then choose Format⇨Advanced⇨Define as Placeholder Text so that the check mark to the left of that option disappears. (You can also press Control+Option+⌘+T.) Now, when you go to a book page that includes the layout text box, when you click in the placeholder text, a blue outline appears around that text (which indicates it's placeholder text) but not around the fixed text. That's a signal to the person working with the text to leave the fixed text alone.

But be careful: That fixed text is still editable. It's just that the placeholder text indicator doesn't include it. If you really want to make fixed text uneditable, put it in its own text box and be sure that its text box is set to be uneditable: In the Layout inspector's Layout pane, deselect the Editable on Pages Using This Layout option.

Portrait versus Landscape Orientation

You may notice in the iBooks Author toolbar the two Orientation icon buttons: one for landscape view and one for portrait view. (You can also toggle between these two views by choosing View⇨Change Orientation or pressing Option+⌘+R.) Remember that an iPad's screen auto-rotates based on how a user is holding it, so applications and their contents need to adjust accordingly.

This dual orientation is a big change for book designers because you're actually working with two layouts in iBooks Author, one for each orientation. iBooks Author handles your basic text flow automatically when a user switches screen orientation, but some elements are treated differently. iBooks Author gives you much more creativity in landscape layouts and pages because most people usually read in that orientation on the iPad.

When creating layouts and pages, you need to think of the landscape and portrait layouts as parallel but separate. So, when you create and modify layouts and pages, start with the landscape orientation, and then switch to the portrait orientation to see how iBooks Author handles your objects and adjust that portrait design as appropriate — for example, you might add different versions of elements you want in both openers.

If you believe dealing with the differences between landscape and portrait orientations is too complicated, you can make an iBooks Author e-book landscape-only. In the Inspector, go to the Document inspector (click the first icon button, which looks like a page), and then select the Disable Portrait Orientation option. You still have all the portrait controls available, but the reader can see the exported book only in landscape orientation on the iPad.

How pages differ

Landscape orientation preserves the notion of pages that you flip through, like you would in a paper book, but portrait orientation treats the entire e-book as one long scroll.

Also, chapter and section layouts in landscape orientation have two pages, whereas portrait layouts have just one. (Page layouts have one page in either layout.)

Here's what each layout displays:

- ✔ **Landscape:** The left page is a unique page template for the start of that chapter or section. The right page is the template for all subsequent added pages.

- ✔ **Portrait:** The chapter or section layout has just one page; that's the scrolling page, in which all the contents appear in the e-book when viewed in portrait orientation. A blue dividing line, as shown in Figure 2-8, is what separates what's unique to the opening page (anything above the line) and what's on all subsequent pages added based on that chapter layout (anything below the line). If you click the line, you can drag it up or down to adjust the boundary between the opening page's unique elements and the common elements for all subsequent pages.

If you try to add widgets, charts, or any other object below the dividing line when in portrait orientation — whether to a layout or a page — they disappear from the layout or page and don't show up in your e-book, even in landscape orientation, so you need to add objects when in landscape orientation. But objects you add above the dividing line when in portrait orientation *do* appear, though just when in portrait orientation.

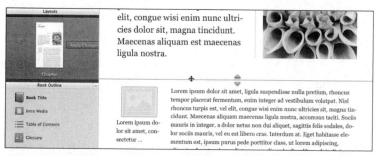

Figure 2-8: In portrait orientation, a dividing line separates the opening page and the subsequent scrolling page.

Where and when objects appear

Portrait orientation removes most objects in your layout from view. Any widgets appear as small icons in the left margin (the *thumbnail track*) of the page, which users can tap to get the full widget. Figure 2-9 shows an example of how iBooks Author repositions and resizes a widget automatically: The Keynote widgets in the landscape layout take half a page width each in the landscape layout, but in the portrait layout, iBooks Author automatically shrinks and moves the widget to the thumbnail track, as Figure 2-9 also shows.

While you add widgets and other captioned objects to your layout, iBooks Author stacks the icons in portrait orientation based on their order in the layout. As Figure 2-10 shows, the icons are stacked together regardless of where the objects appear in the layout. For example, if you have six such objects, with the first on page 2, two on page 4, and three on page 5 in landscape orientation, all six appear at the top of the scrolling page in portrait orientation. That automatic positioning can cause the objects to become divorced from the text that refers to them and to which they add context.

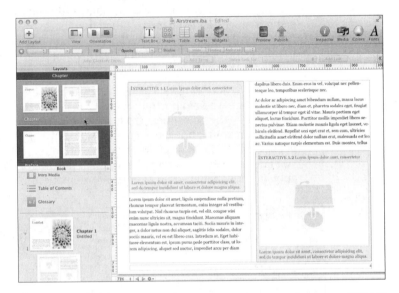

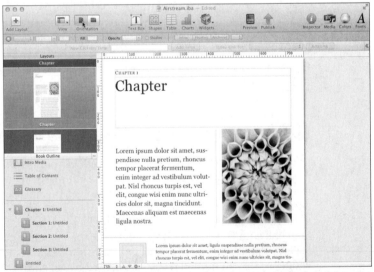

Figure 2-9: A layout in landscape orientation (top) and portrait orientation (bottom).

If you don't want any widgets to appear in portrait view on a page, you can disable their visibility. (Sadly, it's an all-or-nothing proposition.) Open the Inspector by clicking the Inspector button in the toolbar, choosing View⇨Show Inspector, or pressing Option+⌘+I. As shown in Figure 2-11, go to the Layout inspector (click the second icon button from the left in the Inspector) and deselect the Shared with Portrait Layout option (it appears at the bottom if the Book panel is active and about two thirds of the way down from the top if the Layouts panel is active).

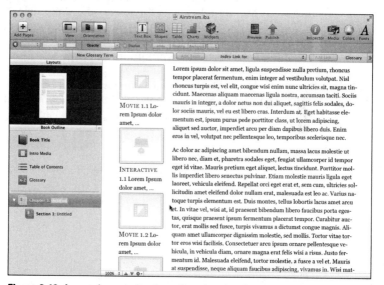

Figure 2-10: A page in portrait orientation, showing the placeholders for widgets and captioned objects.

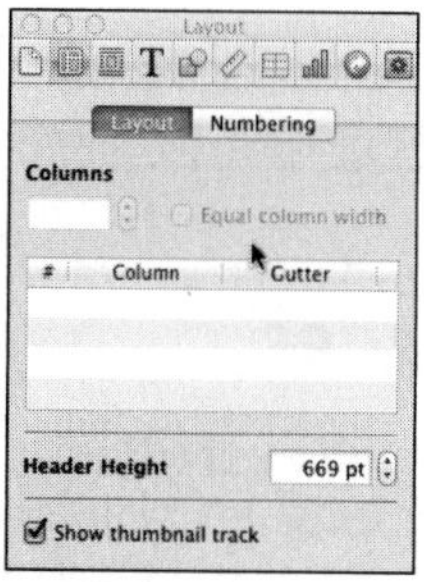

Figure 2-11: The Layout inspector's Layout pane.

Widgets aren't the only objects treated differently between the landscape and portrait orientations. For example, inline shapes, images, charts, and text boxes do appear in both landscape and portrait views, within the mainbar. But floating and anchored objects appear only in landscape orientation — unless they have a caption, in which case, miniature versions appear in the thumbnail track so that users can tap them to open up the full object.

Finally, if you place an object on the first page of a chapter layout in landscape orientation, you can specify whether it appears in portrait orientation by using the Inspector. Make sure you're in landscape orientation, and then go to the Layout inspector (click the second icon button from the left in the Inspector) and deselect the Share with Portrait Layout option, as Figure 2-12 shows.

You don't have this Share with Portrait Layout option available for objects placed on the right page of a chapter layout, on a section or page layout, or on book pages. (Apple's decision in this regard confounds me.)

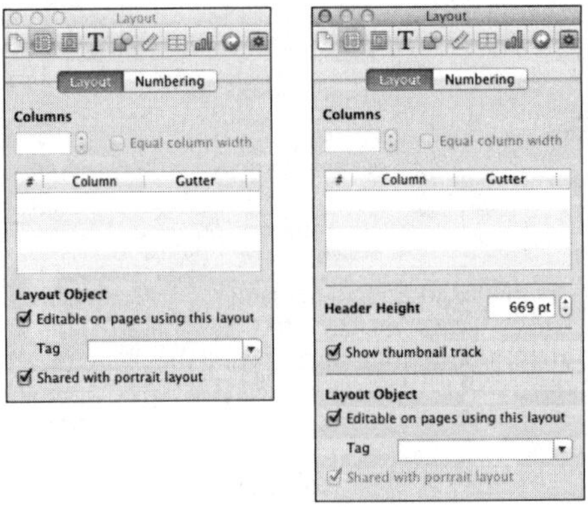

Figure 2-12: The Layout inspector's Layout pane for an image in a landscape chapter layout's first page (left) and for an image in a portrait layout (right).

Different user interfaces

When you're working in portrait orientation, the Book panel doesn't display the page thumbnails available in landscape orientation. Instead, you see just the page, section, and chapter names.

Also, for the reader, the navigation controls change based on whether he's in portrait or landscape orientation, though that doesn't affect your book design or layout work.

Setting the Book Cover

At the top of the Book panel is the Book Title button. Click it to create your book's cover, as Figure 2-13 shows. A typical template has three text boxes — one each for the book series name or other label, the book title, and the author name (or *byline*) — plus a placeholder image. You can edit these objects and add more elements, if desired, by using the techniques described in Chapter 4. (You can add charts, shapes, text boxes, images, and tables, but not widgets.)

Essentially, the book's cover page is a special type of page that you can access through the Book Title button. After you enter the book's actual title text, the button's label changes to match the title's text.

Figure 2-13: Set the book's cover.

Adding an Intro Video, Audio File, or Image

Normally, when a reader on the iPad opens an iBooks Author e-book in iBooks for the first time, the table of contents appears. But you can have a video or audio file play or an image appear first. To do so, click the Intro Media button in the Book panel, and then drag a compatible video, audio, or image file (see Chapter 4) from a folder or disk in the Finder onto the Drop Movie or Image Here area in iBooks Author.

If you use a video or audio file as the e-book's intro, the table of contents appears after the playback has completed. If you use an image, the reader has to manually advance to the table of contents on the iPad. The reader can also manually advance to the table of contents when a video or audio file is playing back, which stops the playback. The method depends on whether the e-book is displayed on the iPad in portrait or landscape mode:

- ✔ **Landscape:** Tap the iPad's screen. You then have three options to advance:

    - Tap the right-arrow button at the bottom-left of the screen.

    - Swipe to the right over the two dots at the bottom-center of the screen.

    - Swipe to the left on the center of the screen. (Reverse the swipe to go back to the intro).

- ✔ **Portrait:** Tap the iPad's screen. A Close box appears at the upper-left corner of the image or video; tap it to close the image or video, and go to the table of contents. You can't stop an audio file this way, however; only in landscape orientation can you interrupt the audio intro to go to the table of contents.

Previewing Your E-Book

While you work on your layout and/or your book's pages, you can preview the book simply by looking at your screen: iBooks Author displays a good facsimile of your book while you work on it, whether in landscape or portrait orientation. But to see how the dynamic capabilities function, you need to preview it on an iPad.

iBooks Author makes that easy. Just follow these steps:

1. **Connect your iPad to your Mac via a USB-to-30-pin cable (the one that came with your iPad).**

2. **Open iBooks on the iPad.**

3. **In iBooks Author on your Mac, click the Preview icon button in the toolbar.**

   Alternatively, you can choose File➪Preview or press Option+⌘+P.

   The first time you do this, you may see a settings sheet that lists your iPad.

4. **If the settings sheet appears, select the iPad (even if its name is grayed out) and click Preview.**

   It can take up to a minute for the e-book to transfer from your Mac to the iPad and then open in iBooks. You can now read the book on the iPad just as a reader would.

The preview version of the e-book stays in the iBooks library — marked with the word Proof over one corner — until you delete it. That way, you don't need to keep the iPad connected to your Mac to review that version.

If you've worked only on the e-book's layout, you need to add at least one chapter to be able to preview it. That chapter need not contain real text and objects, but if it doesn't, you see only place-holder text and objects. If you've worked on the book's pages, you see whatever work you've done.

To see changes to your layout, just send the preview to the iPad again (it must be connected via a USB-to-30-pin cable, of course).

Sometimes, when you have a preview version of the book already open, the updated preview doesn't appear. Just tap the iPad's screen to display the iBooks controls at the top of the screen, and tap the Library button in iBooks to close the e-book and display the iBooks book list. Then send the preview again from your Mac. Likewise, when the iPad is in portrait orientation, the preview may not refresh; just change the iPad's orientation to landscape and try sending the preview from your Mac again.

Another way to preview your e-book is to print it from iBooks Author: Choose File➪Print or press ⌘+P. Of course, a printed version doesn't have any interactivity.

Chapter 3

Working with Text

- -

In This Chapter

▶ Importing text to iBooks Author

▶ Using formatting and styles

▶ Editing and laying out text

- -

Although iBooks Author lets you use a wide variety of objects in your e-books, text forms the basic content of most books. Chances are that your e-books will use a mix of text brought in from a word processor (such as Microsoft Word and Apple Pages) and text entered directly in iBooks Author.

However you get the text into iBooks Author, you edit and format it the same way after it's there. If you use Apple's Pages, the controls for formatting text in iBooks Author should be very familiar. If you use Microsoft Word, the controls use a different approach in many cases: Apple favors its Inspector and drawer mechanisms, whereas Microsoft favors panes, but both are largely contextual. And what they accomplish is largely the same.

But bringing text in from outside has implications about its formatting, so take some time to figure out an appropriate workflow for your text preparation, as I explain in this chapter.

Working with Outside Text

Layout programs for print books let you create a template with containers for your text, like iBooks Author does (see Chapter 2). But they let you import text from document files into those containers so that imported text flows through those predefined containers.

iBooks Author works a little differently to achieve that result, so if you're experienced in print-oriented tools such as Adobe InDesign and QuarkXPress, be sure to pay close attention to how iBooks Author works for file import.

Supported formats and methods

For importing document files, iBooks Author can open Microsoft Word files (both the .doc and .docx versions) and Apple Pages files.

You can also drag RTF (Rich Text Format) documents and text-only files (.txt, .html, .htm, and other unformatted ASCII files) into iBooks Author. (The white + [plus sign] symbol in a green circle appears near the pointer if the item can be placed in iBooks Author, as shown in Figure 3-1.) The text is inserted into an existing text box if you release the pointer over a text box. A new text box is created if you release the pointer outside a text box.

For copying and pasting, you can copy text from any application that lets you select and then copy or cut text, though text formatting is preserved only if you copy from Word or Pages.

To import a Word or Pages document, follow these steps:

1. **Choose Insert⇨Chapter from Pages or Word Document.**

   A settings sheet appears, where you can choose the document.

2. **Select a document, and then click the Insert button.**

   A second settings sheet appears, showing thumbnails of the available layouts.

3. **Click the layout that you want to apply.**

   You can access more layouts than initially appear in the settings sheet; just scroll through the list to see them.

4. **(Optional) Select the Preserve Document Paragraph Styles on Import option.**

   If selected, this option loads the paragraph and character styles defined in the imported Word or Pages document. (The following section explains the issues of using and not using imported styles.)

5. **Click the Choose button to import the document.**

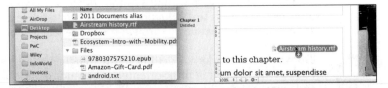

Figure 3-1: Dragging an RTF file into iBooks Author to create a new text box based on that file.

As noted in Chapter 2, importing such a file creates a new chapter at the end of your e-book, based on the layout you choose during import. All text flows in the mainbar space defined in the chapter layout.

Any embedded graphics and tables in the imported Word and Pages files are imported as inline objects, and text boxes are imported as anchored objects. Document settings such as columns, headers, and footers are ignored, as are comments and cross-references. Footnote numbers are preserved but not their actual footnotes. (iBooks Author doesn't support footnotes, a very odd omission for an authoring tool aimed at textbook publishers.) Hyperlinks are also preserved, but links to internal bookmarks likely won't work correctly.

What you can't do, as other layout programs do, is import a file into an existing iBooks Author chapter, section, page, or text box. To do so, you need to paste the text instead from Word, Pages, or other text-editing program.

Issues with imported files' styles

Typically, when you do your text editing in a program such as Word or Pages, you format the text in that program, applying styles to various types of paragraphs and text selections, as well as using local formatting attributes such as boldface and superscripts. Print-oriented applications such as InDesign and QuarkXPress note the styles used in the source files and then apply the same-named styles in their documents, thus applying their styles to the imported text. It's a very handy way to ensure consistent, correct formatting.

But iBooks Author doesn't handle styles so nicely for imported files. (This is also an issue in Apple Pages, on which iBooks Author's text capabilities are based.) If you've defined styles in iBooks Author and import a Word or Pages file that uses styles with the same names, iBooks Author doesn't apply its versions of those styles to the imported text. Instead, it preserves the styles of the source files. That means you have to update the imported text in iBooks Author manually — which can take a lot of work, depending on how your text is styled. And each time you import a document (such as for each chapter in your book), you have the same issue of needing to fix that text's styles.

You could import your document without retaining its style information, but that can cause even more work: All text is given the style applied to your placeholder mainbar text, so you then have to identify all text that should have special styles applied, such as headlines, and manually reapply them. You do get a slight clue about what text might have these exceptions: The text size and local formatting (boldface, italics, small caps, and so on) of the imported text is preserved, even though its font and style names aren't, so you can look for such visual variances to figure out the text to which you want to apply styles.

If you copy and paste text from another program — even if you use the option to retain formatting (choose Edit⇨Paste and Retain Style or press Option+Shift+⌘+V) — all your text has the paragraph style Free Form applied to it, with the retained formatting converted to local formatting that you'll want to override with paragraph and character styles in iBooks Author. Any RTF text dragged into iBooks Author also has its text tagged as Free Form and all its styles converted to local formatting. (Text-only files have no formatting that needs to be converted.)

In the section "Defining and Applying Styles," later in this chapter, I explain how to define and apply styles in iBooks Author.

Recommended workflows

Although you can write and edit your book from scratch in iBooks Author, you probably want to do your writing and editing in Microsoft Word or Apple Pages — even with the cleanup work on formatting that iBooks Author requires for such imported text. You can more easily edit and format text in those programs. Plus, because iBooks Author runs only on the Mac, the only way for Windows users to contribute to the book is to use Word.

If revisions tracking is critical — such as for files that are written by one person, edited by a second, and copy-edited and proofed by a third, where you want to know what each person has changed — you have to use Word or Pages because iBooks Author can't track revisions. Only after you finalize the content of the files do you bring them into iBooks Author.

Even if your process is less elaborate — for example, if you're a teacher creating lessons or guides for your students — you might want to do the majority of your text work in Word or Pages because they're designed to let you focus on the words, whereas iBooks Author's interface is oriented to layout work, so your working window for text is constrained. (If you switch to portrait orientation, though, you can better approximate the way you work with text in Word or Pages.)

If you do your primary text work in a program other than iBooks Author, note that iBooks Author supports just the limited set of fonts in iBooks on the iPad. This set includes many familiar web fonts used by most browsers and another group of Apple-supplied fonts. If you use other fonts in Word or Pages, iBooks Author substitutes its own fonts during import, but for simplicity, you might want to use the same fonts in Word or Pages that iBooks Author uses. When you install iBooks Author, its fonts are also installed on your Mac, so they're available to Word and Pages. (If you do your work in Windows for transfer to a Mac later, you won't have access to all these iBooks Author fonts, of course.)

Because iBooks Author isn't good at managing styles during importing, the path to the least amount of rework is to import all your chapter files in Word or Pages format *before* working on applying the correct styles. That way, you do the style fix-it work just once.

The more your words are related to your visual layout, the more it makes sense to do all the work in iBooks Author. For example, if you're doing a field guide in which the emphasis is on photos and diagrams, and the text is short and tied to the images, it makes more sense to lay out the images, then write the text to fit.

Although iBooks Author doesn't support revisions tracking — so you can't monitor, and then approve or override, the text changes made by someone else — iBooks Author does let you peruse previous versions of your file so that you can restore previous text and objects, if desired — a standard capability in software optimized for Mac OS X Lion. To peruse such previous versions, choose File⇨Revert Document, and then click the Browse Versions button in the full-screen window that appears. Figure 3-2 shows the versions interface that you use to navigate previous versions. *Note:* You can't access the previous versions of an iBooks Author file in a copy of that file or if the file's been moved from its original location.

Whatever the appropriate workflow for your e-book, you'll produce the visual elements and the interactive elements outside iBooks Author. To make things easier, place them in a project folder so that they're all in one place when it comes time to import them.

If you're using Word or Pages to do your text, place your photos, screenshots, and other such bitmapped images in your document file as inline graphics in otherwise-empty paragraphs; iBooks Author then automatically places your images into your text as inline objects when you import the file.

And even if you decide you want these imported inline graphics to be *anchored objects* (where objects align to the top or bottom of columns on the page their text appears) or to be floating objects to create cleaner layouts, you can easily convert the imported inline objects in iBooks Author to anchored or floating objects after they're imported. (Chapter 2 explains inline, anchored, and floating objects.) By starting with them as inline objects imported from your Word or Pages file, at least they're relatively close to where you ultimately want them, so you don't have to search for their text references when you want to figure out where to place them in the layout.

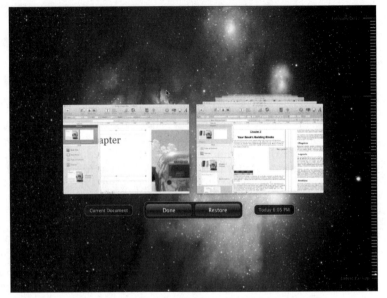

Figure 3-2: Navigating previous versions of an iBooks Author document.

Applying Text Formatting

iBooks Author has the kinds of text formatting controls you'd expect, similar to those in Microsoft Word and Apple Pages. If you apply formatting through styles, as explained in the section "Defining and Applying Styles," later in this chapter, you can maintain consistent formatting and save effort when you update your formatting, but you can also apply them directly to selected text (doing so is called *local formatting*). Either way, you're working with the same formatting attributes.

Most text formatting options are available in one of two places:

- ✔ **Format bar:** This bar appears beneath the toolbar when you select text or place the pointer within text. See Figure 3-3.

- ✔ **Format menu:** Its Font submenu lets you format text selections, and the Text submenu lets you format paragraphs.

If the Format bar isn't visible, display it by choosing View⇨Show Format Bar or pressing Shift+⌘+R; the same methods also hide the Format bar.

Figure 3-3: The Format bar (at bottom).

Character formatting

iBooks Author provides a variety of formatting options for text selections, including font, font style, text size, color, various typographic controls, and language (for use in spell-checking and hyphenation).

Font

iBooks Author supports a variety of typefaces (popularly called *fonts*) for your text. iBooks Author can use only the fonts in its Fonts menu, which are the fonts available in iBooks on the iPad. (Apple periodically changes its font mix on the iPad, so you may see the font list in iBooks Author change as well over time as the software is updated.)

To apply fonts, use the Format bar's Font pop-up menu, which shows the currently selected text's font name (Georgia, in Figure 3-3). By default, it shows the font name in its actual font, but you can turn that feature off by following these steps:

1. **Choose iBooks Author⇨Preferences.**

   Alternatively, you can press ⌘+, (comma).

   The Preferences dialog box appears, displaying the General pane.

2. **Deselect the Show Font Preview in Format Bar Font Menu option.**

3. **Click the Close box.**

You can choose Format⇨Font⇨Show Fonts or press ⌘+T to open the Fonts panel. (The Show Fonts option is also available in the contextual menu that appears if you Control-click or right-click text.)

Avoid using the Fonts panel because it displays all fonts available on your Mac, including fonts not supported on the iPad; these fonts look okay in iBooks Author on your Mac but not in the e-book in the iPad's iBooks. Use the Format bar's Font pop-up menu, instead.

Font style

Most fonts come with variations known as font styles, such as boldface and italics, which you can apply to text. (The font style is set to Regular in Figure 3-3.) A related set of formatting attributes is also available: underline, strikethrough, and outline.

Several font styles are available by choosing Format⇨Font or via the Font Styles pop-up menu in the Format bar: boldface, italics, and underlining. You can quickly apply (as well as remove) boldface, italics, or underlining in several ways:

- ✔ Choose Format⇨Font, and then choose the appropriate option in the submenu that appears.
- ✔ Click the **B**, *I*, or U̲ icon button in the Format bar.
- ✔ Press the keyboard shortcuts ⌘+B, ⌘+I, or ⌘+U.

Two types of font styles — strikethrough and outline — are available only if you choose Format⇨Font and then select the appropriate option from the submenu that appears.

Text size

Text size helps distinguish different elements, especially in a hierarchy, such as using the largest size for your titles, the next-largest for headings, and so on. (The text size is 24 in Figure 3-3.) You can apply sizes in increments of a tenth of a point, though it's rare to use anything but whole points.

To apply text size, choose one of the common sizes from the Text Size pop-up menu in the Format bar or enter a specific size in the Text Size pop-up menu's text field. You can also make the text bigger one point at a time by choosing Format⇨Font⇨Bigger or pressing ⌘+= (equal sign), or make it smaller by choosing Format⇨Font⇨Smaller or pressing ⌘+− (hyphen).

iBooks Author displays a + (plus sign) rather than an = (equal sign) in its Bigger menu option, but you don't need to press the Shift key to make the text bigger, which you would to get the actual + (plus sign) character.

Color

You can apply color to both text and its background. To do so, use the two color swatches on the Format bar, to the right of the Text Size pop-up menu; the Text Color swatch (on the left) applies color to the text and the Background Color swatch (on the right) applies color to the background. The A character in the Text Color swatch represents the currently selected text, and its color represents the currently applied color to that text. In both swatches, a diagonal gray line superimposed on the swatch means no color (the None color) is applied. (In Figure 3-3, the text color is black and the background color is None.)

You can also use the Inspector to adjust the text and background colors, as shown in Figure 3-4: You set the text color in the Text inspector's Text pane's Color & Alignment section and the text background in the More pane's Background Fills section.

Typographic formatting

Print publishing uses four specialized types of typographic formatting that iBooks Author also supports — just choose Format➪Font to access these formats through the submenu that appears. The first two formatting controls are meant to provide a more pleasing visual experience through subtle text enhancements, and the second two are more commonly used for meaning and emphasis:

- ✔ **Tracking:** Also called *character spacing,* this submenu's options adjust the space between letters; the options are None, Tighten, and Loosen. The None setting usually works just fine for e-books, but you may adjust tracking due to personal preferences or for visual effect (for example, a popular technique is to put all-cap text labels on colored backgrounds and space out the letters). You can also use the Text inspector to adjust the tracking, as shown in Figure 3-4.

- ✔ **Ligature:** The options in this submenu substitute special characters for certain letter sequences that can look awkward when using the standard characters. For example, rather than use the fi letters, a more pleasing presentation is to use the fi ligature (see how the *i*'s dot merges into the *f*'s curve?). The options are None, Use Common, and Use All. The common ligatures are for the letter sequences *fi, fl, ffi,* and *ffl;* some fonts have additional ligatures, such as for *ts* — and some fonts don't have any ligatures available (usually web fonts such as Georgia and Times New Roman). Furthermore, ligatures aren't used for text that have loose spacing because the intent is to merge two letters that normally have elements that come very close, so there's no awkward abutment of those elements. You can turn off ligatures for selected text by using the Remove Ligatures option in the Text inspector's More pane, shown in Figure 3-4.

- ✔ **Baseline:** This submenu's options provide two types of controls:
  - *Superscript and subscript:* Reduces the text size and repositions the character (such as for footnotes, physics labels, and mathematical equations)
  - *Baseline shift:* Raises or lowers the character without changing its size

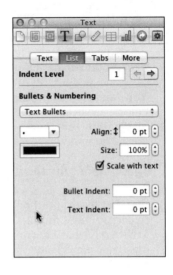

Figure 3-4: The four formatting panes in the Text inspector: Text, List, Tabs, and More.

In the Baseline submenu, the options are Superscript (you can also press Control+⌘+= [equal sign]), Subscript (Control+⌘+– [hyphen]), Raise, and Lower. When you raise or lower text, iBooks Author moves it up or down one point at a time. You can also use the Text inspector to adjust the baseline, as shown in Figure 3-4.

✔ **Capitalization:** This submenu lets you change the capitalization of your text. The options are

- *None:* Uses whatever capitalization you typed.
- *All Caps:* Capitalizes every letter in the selected text.
- *Small Caps:* Uses a reduced-size capital letter in place of lowercase letters.
- *Title Case:* Capitalizes the first letter of each word.

Title Case indiscriminately capitalizes all words' first letters, but most stylebooks recommend capitalizing all nouns, adjectives, adverbs, and verbs — but (unless they're the first or last word in the title) not articles, prepositions, or conjunctions.

Language

You can apply a language to text selections. Although the language applied doesn't change the text's appearance, it does tell iBooks Author how to check the spelling of and hyphenate the text, so it can be an important formatting option to set in multilingual publishing — especially as part of a paragraph style or character style.

To set the selected text's language, go to the Text inspector's More pane and choose the language from the Language pop-up menu. (*Note:* English means American English.) By default, iBooks Author applies the language to which your Mac is set. The Language pop-up menu has two special options:

✔ **None:** Disables spell checking and hyphenation.

✔ **All:** Has iBooks Author try to figure out the language for each word by checking in its dictionaries.

The All option makes sense for paragraphs that contain common foreign phrases from multiple languages, but it's best to apply the native language in most cases.

Paragraph formatting

iBooks Author provides the formatting options for paragraphs that I discuss in the following sections; these options apply to the entire paragraph, no matter what text you may have selected in it. You can apply most of the paragraph formatting in the Text inspector and its four panes, shown in Figure 3-4. To open the inspector

- ✔ Click the Inspector button in the toolbar.

- ✔ Choose View➪Show Inspector.

- ✔ Press Option+⌘+I, and then click the Text icon button (the T icon).

You can also apply alignment and indentation by choosing Format➪ Text or by using the keyboard shortcuts noted in the following section, and you can apply alignment, line spacing, and lists via the Format bar.

Alignment and indentation

Most text in a book is aligned to the left margin, and it can also be aligned to the right margin. When aligned only to the left margin, the text is *left-aligned* or *ragged right;* when aligned to both margins, it's *justified.* Text can also be *right-aligned* to just the right margin or centered between the two margins.

You can align paragraphs in a variety of ways:

- ✔ Choose Format➪Text and then choose Align Left, Center, Align Right, or Justify from the submenu.

- ✔ Use these keyboard shortcuts:

  - *Align Left:* Shift+⌘+[

  - *Center:* Shift+⌘+\

  - *Align Right:* Shift+⌘+]

  - *Justify:* Option+Shift+⌘+\

  The iBooks Author menus for these options display ⌘+\ rather than Shift+⌘+\, ⌘+{ rather than Shift+⌘+[, and ⌘+} rather than Shift+⌘+]. Apple assumes you realize these characters need the Shift key pressed, but this book doesn't make that assumption and instead spells out all the required keys.

- ✔ Click one of the four alignment icon buttons in the Format bar or in the Text inspector's Text pane.

A related control is indentation, for which iBooks Author provides three types that can be used singly or together:

✔ **Block indent:** Moves the entire paragraph in from the left margin. You typically use block indents to set off extended quotes (called *block quotes*) or in outlines to show relative levels:

- Choose Format⇨Text⇨Increase List Indent Level or press ⌘+], to indent the text. Each time you do this for a text selection, the text is further indented.

- Choose Format⇨Text⇨Decrease List Indent Level or press ⌘+[to decrease the indentation. Each time you do this for a text selection, the text is further un-indented.

You can also use the Indent Level icon buttons in the Text inspector's List pane. You don't need to make the paragraph into a bulleted or number list to apply block indents.

✔ **Paragraph indent:** Specifies a left and/or right indentation for a paragraph in terms of points. In traditional publishing, this is the usual mechanism for specifying block quotes. You set this indent in the Text inspector's Tabs pane.

✔ **First-line indents:** Specifies how much the first line of a paragraph is inset from its left margin, in points. You set this indent in the Text inspector's Tabs pane.

Typically, you use a first-line indent only when your paragraphs have no extra space before or after them. The reader usually needs just one visual clue, not two, to let him know when a new paragraph has begun.

Line spacing

Known as *leading* to publishers, line spacing controls how close lines of text are to each other within a column or text box. You set line spacing in increments of one line, so a setting of 1.5 provides a half line of space between lines. The actual measurement of a half line depends on the current text size.

To apply line spacing, you have several options:

✔ Choose a value from the Line Spacing menu in the Format bar. (The menu displays the current line spacing value, and it has a double-arrow icon to its left.)

✔ Access the Text inspector's Text pane. This pane provides the Line slider, a text field, and stepper controls to adjust the line spacing.

✔ Also in the Text inspector's Text pane, use the pop-up menu below the Line text field to choose Single or Double (rather than enter 1 or 2) or to choose Multiple (which defaults to the last line spacing you specified).

If you've used desktop publishing tools such as InDesign and QuarkXPress, you're used to specifying line spacing precisely in points, but iBooks Author instead uses the notion of line increments common to Microsoft Word and Apple Pages by default. You can specify line spacing in terms of points by choosing Exactly, At Least, or Between from the pop-up menu below the Line text field. The option you choose determines how the spacing is applied:

✔ **Exactly:** Ensures that all lines are spaced apart by the number of points specified in the Line text field, even if some elements in the line might overlap with adjacent lines

✔ **At Least:** Ensures that no less than the space specified in the Line text field is used — but if you have superscripts or elements that are larger than the normal text in a line, extra space is added to avoid overlap with adjacent lines

✔ **Between:** Applies the amount of space specified in the Line text field to be used between lines, which can cause it to vary if lines have larger-than-normal objects in them

Most documents should use one of the line-spacing increments or the Exactly option to prevent distracting variation in line spacing. You may want to use At Least or Between in documents that contain complex scientific or mathematical formulas that might take one or more lines but need to be in the text itself, rather than broken off into a figure.

Paragraph spacing

If you're not using first-line indents to indicate when a new paragraph has begun, you should use paragraph spacing to provide that visual indication. But even if you use first-line indents for your text, you may want to use paragraph spacing in other text, such as before headings, to help make their sections more visibly separate from the text that precedes them.

Whatever your purpose for adding space above or below a paragraph, you specify the spacing in the Text inspector's Text pane, using the Before Paragraph and After Paragraph controls. You can use whichever method you prefer — the sliders, the text fields, or the stepper controls — to adjust the spacing.

Tabs

iBooks Author's control over tabs are in the Text inspector's Tabs pane. They're the standard controls you'd expect — the position, alignment, leader text (often a row of periods) between the tab positions, and character used to indicate a decimal point for tabs that align to the decimal. (North Americans use periods as the decimal point, but Europeans tend to use commas.) To add a tab stop, click the + (plus sign) icon button; to remove a tab stop, select it from the list and click the – (minus sign) icon button.

You can see the tab stops for the current paragraph indicated in the ruler below the toolbar (and below the Format bar and Glossary bar, if they're visible), as Figure 3-5 shows. (If you don't see the ruler, choose View⇨Show Layout Boundaries or press Shift+⌘+L.)

The ruler works just like the ones in Word and Pages: You can drag tab stops on it to reposition them, as well as drag them off the ruler to remove them. Click in the ruler to add a tab stop. Double-click a tab stop to change it to a different alignment (each time you double-click it, its icon changes to reflect the next available option).

Figure 3-5: The ruler (at bottom).

Hyphenation

By default, iBooks Author enables hyphenation for text — when a word has to be broken up to fit the first half at the end of a line and the last half at the beginning of the next line, for example. If you don't want text hyphenation (such as for titles and headings), turn it off for the current paragraph in the Text inspector's More pane by selecting the Remove Hyphenation for Paragraph option.

iBooks Author doesn't offer a command or special character to disable hyphenation for individual words, like you can find in desktop publishing programs. Nor can you specify hyphenation rules, such as the maximum number of consecutive hyphenated lines or the minimum number of letters before or after a hyphen.

Break and keep settings

In the Text inspector's More pane, you can specify how a paragraph may break across columns and text boxes to accommodate how your text flows.

Normally, the text fills the current column or text box, then continues to the next column or text box. But that approach can lead to awkward situations, such as a heading appearing at the bottom with its related text on the next column or text box. Or a heading might break across columns or text boxes. Or you may get unsightly results known as widows and orphans; a *widow* is the last line of a paragraph appearing at the top of a column or text box, and an *orphan* is the first line of a paragraph appearing at the bottom of a column or text box.

Widows are considered more unsightly than orphans because they often take up just part of the line, creating an awkward gap at the top of the column or text box.

There are four options for controlling how paragraphs break and stay together:

- ✔ **Keep Lines Together:** Prevents a paragraph from breaking across columns or text boxes.

- ✔ **Keep with Following Paragraph:** Doesn't allow paragraphs, such as headlines, to be separated from the paragraph that follows.

- ✔ **Paragraph Starts on New Page:** Forces a page break before the current paragraph, such as for use with top-level headings. (You can manually force a page break by choosing Insert⇨Page Break, and you can manually force a column break by choosing Insert⇨Column Break.)

- ✔ **Prevent Widow and Orphan Lines:** Ensures that no column or text box ends with the first line of a paragraph and that no column or text box begins with the last line of a paragraph. Instead, every column or text box has at least two lines at the top or bottom. Note that, unlike desktop publishing apps, you can't separately control widows and orphans in iBooks Author.

Lists

A common paragraph-formatting device is the list, whether numbered or bulleted. iBooks Author treats lists as a separate type of formatting because the list formats don't affect the other paragraph formatting you may have set.

You can apply several types of popular list formats to paragraphs: bulleted, numbered, and tiered numbered. (A tiered numbered list uses 1 for the top level, 1.1 for its first sublevel, 1.1.1 for its first sub-sublevel, and so on.) You can apply several common list formats from the Format bar's List Style icon menu (the icon for this menu looks like a bulleted list), or you can use the Text inspector's List pane to choose from all the available options.

When you use the List pane, you can choose two types of numbered lists: Text Bullets and Image Bullets. For text bullets, you can choose the specific bullet character and its color. For text and image bullets, you can choose its size and alignment relative to the text, as well as specify both the bullet's indent from the margin and the text's indent from the margin (to achieve that hanging-text look). The Image Bullet option uses a sphere graphic supplied by Apple. If you want to use your own graphic as the bullet, choose Custom Image instead, select an image in the Open dialog box that appears, and click Open to insert it.

When working with numbered lists and tiered numbered lists, your options are the same: You can choose the numbering style (such as 1, 2, 3; A, B, C; or i, ii, iii), as well as specify both the numeral's indent from the margin and the text's indent from the margin (again, to achieve that hanging-text look). You can also set whether the paragraph's numbering picks up from the last numbered item (which may not be adjacent to this paragraph) or starts at a number you specify.

Defining and Applying Styles

Using styles is a critical task in creating an e-book. If you're new to publishing, however, it's a task you may not think of doing: Many people simply highlight their text in programs such as Word and Pages, and then apply the desired local formatting (such as font, capitalization, and text size) to it. But that means everything has to be selected again if you change the design and need to apply a different font or size. It's simply too much work for a book-length project.

The use of styles gets rid of that unnecessary work, and it ensures consistent formatting across the entire book. Rather than apply each of the desired local formats to text, you apply a single style that contains all that formatting. And if you change the style, all the text it's applied to is automatically updated to use the new formatting.

The three types of styles

You can define and apply three kinds of styles:

- ✔ **Paragraph styles:** Apply to the entire paragraph and include both text-formatting attributes, such as font and size, and paragraph-formatting attributes, such as alignment and margins. (I explain this kind of formatting in the section "Paragraph formatting," earlier in this chapter.)

✔ **List styles:** Apply the bulleted or numbered list formatting described in the section "Lists," earlier in this chapter. List styles don't retain other formatting information, so these styles affect only the list attributes, not formatting such as keep options (see the "Break and keep settings" section, earlier in this chapter) and fonts (see the "Font" section, earlier in this chapter). Typically, lists' paragraphs should have both a paragraph style and a list style applied.

✔ **Character styles:** Apply to just the text you select. A character style overrides the paragraph style wherever its attributes differ from that paragraph style. For example, in a bulleted list, you might want the first phrase after each bullet to be bold and blue, and use the Arial font. Your paragraph style might use the Times New Roman font at normal weight, at 12-point size, with the color black, aligned left, and with a first-line indent. You would apply the character style to the first phrase in each bullet, which would change the font to Arial, the weight to bold, and the color to blue but leave the size, alignment, and indent unchanged.

The style drawer

When working with styles, you should open the style drawer, which lists all the available styles. You can open or close (hide) this drawer in several ways:

✔ Click the blue Style Drawer icon button at the far-left of the Format bar.

✔ Choose View➪Style Drawer.

✔ Press Shift+⌘+T.

Figure 3-6 shows the style drawer; it can appear at the right or left of the main application window. Initially, it appears on the side that has the most room. After that, it continues to appear on that side unless it no longer has enough room, in which case, it appears on the other side (if that side has enough room). If it doesn't have enough room on either side, it doesn't appear.

In the style drawer, paragraph styles are always visible. You can show and hide character styles and list styles by clicking the two icon buttons at the bottom-right of the style drawer.

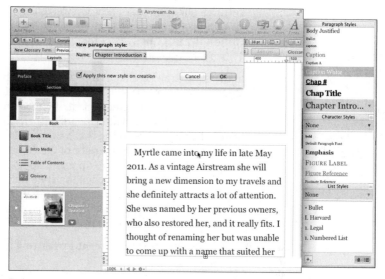

Figure 3-6: The style drawer and dialog box that appear when you create a new style.

Defining styles

To define a style, follow these steps:

1. **Format a paragraph or text selection with all the attributes you want to be included in the paragraph or character style.**

   To define a list style, you want the paragraph to have your list settings applied.

2. **Select the text with the formatting that you want to convert into a style.**

   For character styles, you need to select at least one character. For paragraph styles, you can either select the text or simply insert the pointer anywhere in the paragraph.

3. **Create a new style.**

   You can use one of these two methods:

   - At the bottom of the style drawer, click and hold the + (plus sign) icon button to open an icon menu that displays a list of three style types that you can choose from (Paragraph, Character, and List). If you just click the icon button like any other button, iBooks Author assumes you want to create a paragraph style. A settings sheet appears (shown in Figure 3-6), where you enter a name for the style in the Name text field. Optionally but highly recommended, select the Apply This New Style on Creation check box. Then click OK.

- In the style drawer, click the down-pointing triangle icon in whichever style list you want to create the style for: Paragraph, Character, or List. If you've modified an existing style, the triangle appears to the right of the affected style's name. If the text has no style applied, the triangle appears to the right of the None style. When you click the triangle, a pop-up menu appears. (You can also Control-click or right-click the style name to get the same options via the contextual menu.) Choose the Create New Style from Selection option. You now have a new style with the selected text's attributes.

iBooks Author picks up the current formatting and uses it in that new style.

After you create a style, you can assign it a keyboard shortcut (what iBooks Author calls a *hot key*). In the pop-up menu or contextual menu for that style, choose Hot Key and then the desired function key (F1 through F8) from the submenu, or choose None to remove a previously assigned hot key.

Applying styles

To apply a paragraph or list style — also called *tagging* — click anywhere in a paragraph and click the desired style from the style drawer. You can also apply a style from the Format bar by using the Paragraph Style menu (the ¶) and Character Style menu (the A) at the far-left and the List Style menu (which looks like a bulleted list) at the far-right. If you defined a hot key for the style, use it to apply the style; in some cases, you may need to also press and hold the Fn key because the function keys are often used by other Mac OS X functions.

For paragraphs, iBooks Author overrides any paragraph style previously applied, but it leaves previously applied character styles and local formatting such as italics, as they were. Character styles override both previously applied character styles and local formatting for the selected text. And list styles override just the list settings for the paragraph.

iBooks Author also lets you copy local formatting from one text selection or paragraph to another. It's not really a form of styles, but iBooks Author uses the term *styles* when referring to what other programs call *format painting*.

To copy the formatting applied to a text selection, follow these steps:

1. **Choose Format⇨Copy Character Style.**

   Alternatively, you can press Option+Shift+⌘+C.

   If the selected text doesn't have local formatting applied, you can't copy its formatting, and this command doesn't do anything.

2. **Select the text to which you want to apply that formatting.**

3. **Choose Format⇨Paste Character Style.**

   Or press Option+⌘+V.

   The formatting you copied is applied to the text you selected when you pasted that formatting.

To copy the formatting of a particular paragraph, follow these steps:

1. **Choose Format⇨Copy Paragraph Style.**

   Alternatively, press Option+⌘+C

   If the selected text doesn't have local formatting applied, you can't copy its formatting, and this command does nothing.

2. **Place the mouse cursor in the paragraph to which you want to apply that formatting.**

3. **Choose Format⇨Paste Paragraph Style.**

   Or press Option+⌘+V.

   The formatting you copied is applied to the text you selected when you pasted that formatting.

Modifying styles and their tagged text

To modify a style, you have to first modify text currently tagged with that style. When the style drawer is open, you can tell what styles are applied to the current text because they're highlighted with a light blue background.

After you modify the style, the down-pointing triangle next to its name in the style drawer turns red, which indicates the text's formatting deviates from the style's settings. Click the triangle and choose Redefine Style for Selection in the pop-up menu that appears to update the style's definition. (You can also Control-click or right-click the style name to get the same options via a contextual menu.) All text that uses that style is now updated to the new formatting.

If you want to make the deviantly formatted text conform to the original style, choose Revert to Defined Style from the pop-up menu instead. (For paragraph styles, this option also removes character styles and local formatting applied to the paragraph.) And if you want to create a new style from the variant, choose Create New Style from Selection.

Another option in the style drawer from that pop-up menu is Select All Uses of *Style Name*. You use this option to apply an iBooks Author style to text imported from Word or Pages, or pasted from another source. For example, if your book has defined the mainbar text's paragraph style as Mainbar Text but the imported file uses the name Body Text, you can use this option to select all the Body Text–tagged paragraphs and then apply Mainbar Text to them.

Likewise, if the imported file has a style named Normal that differs from your book's definition of Normal style, use the Select All Using *Style Name* option to select all text in the book that uses that style name — both text created in iBooks Author and text imported — and then apply the book's Normal to all of it.

You might wonder why you can't just use the Revert to Defined Style option instead after selecting all text that uses the Normal style. Unfortunately, doing so reverts the formatting only in the paragraph your cursor is in, not all the selected text. So, if you import text from Word or Pages, do it all at the same time, then refine your formatting and styles so that you can apply them all in one fell swoop, and add original text in iBooks Author only when you get the imported text properly formatted.

Deleting styles

To delete a style, Control-click or right-click its name in the style drawer and choose Delete Style from the contextual menu that appears. If the style is in use in your book, you must apply a replacement style — a dialog box appears where you choose the style you want to use.

Editing Text

Editing text in iBooks Author works like editing text in pretty much any application. You click in a text box (or double-click in a shape) to insert the text cursor, and then you can add or delete text; or select text, and then use any of the standard Mac OS X methods to copy, cut, and paste it. But iBooks Author offers you some specialized capabilities that you can do, in addition to the usual editing.

Placeholder text

As explained in Chapter 2, your iBooks Author layout templates provide text boxes and other objects that you can use on each page based on that template. There are two kinds of such elements:

- ✔ **Standard content:** Contents appear on each page exactly as they do in the template element.

- ✔ **Placeholders:** Contents are merely placeholders for the book author to modify.

For example, your layout might have a text box containing the name of the current chapter and the current page number (called *folios* by publishers). (A special type of placeholder text automatically updates itself, such as for the current page number or chapter number. Chapter 7 explains how to insert such metadata-based text.) Or it might have a shape or image used as an emblem on each chapter's opening page, such as a school logo. Such elements are fixed in the template and not meant to be edited on the book's pages by the author.

But your layout almost always will have a placeholder text box for each page's mainbar, and probably a placeholder image for your chapter opener; in these cases, you do want the author to change the content on the book pages.

You can edit all text in a placeholder text box on the book's pages. For example, you might have a text box for the author's byline that says By Author Name Here. When editing that placeholder text, you can easily select all the contents (by choosing Edit⇨Select All or pressing ⌘+A), and then type in **By** and the author's name (you lose the By part when you select all the contents).

If your layout can use separate text boxes for such situations (such as a fixed one for By followed by an adjacent placeholder one for Author's Name Here), it should. But it's not always possible to use such a combination of fixed and placeholder text boxes. So, when editing placeholder text, be careful that all the text you want to appear is there.

Cut, delete, copy, and paste

Like any Mac application, iBooks Author supports the standard cut, delete, copy, and paste operations:

✔ **Cut:** Choose Edit➪Cut or press ⌘+X.

✔ **Delete:** Choose Edit➪Delete or press Delete (you can't paste text deleted this way, like you can with cut text).

✔ **Copy:** Choose Edit➪Copy or press ⌘+C.

✔ **Paste:** Choose Edit➪Paste or press ⌘+V.

iBooks Author has an alternative paste command, as well: Choose Edit➪Paste and Match Style (or press Option+Shift+⌘+V). Just to confuse matters, that menu option can also appear as Paste and Retain Style. You get Paste and Match Style when pasting text onto a page, rather than into a text box; pasting onto the page creates a text box for that text. You get Paste and Retain Style when pasting into existing text. The two commands work differently, even though they share a keyboard shortcut.

When you paste text onto a page, the normal Paste command retains the original text's formatting, whereas Paste and Match Style uses the default text formatting for a new text box. (You set this default style by formatting text as desired in a text box, then choosing Format➪Advanced➪Define Default Text Box Style. This style picks up not just the text's formatting, but also the text box's formatting, described in the section "Laying Out Text," later in this chapter, and in Chapter 4.)

When you paste text into existing text or into an empty text box, the normal Paste command reformats the pasted text to match the style of the text into which you're pasting it (or to the default style for that text box, if it has no other text in it). But Paste and Retain Style keeps the pasted text's original formatting intact.

Search and replace

You can search and replace text in your book; iBooks Author provides a typical Find & Replace dialog box (choose Edit➪Find➪Find or press ⌘+F) where you enter the find-and-replace terms, and then replace them all at the same time or go through each occurrence to selectively replace the term.

Searches look for text only in your book pages, not in your layouts.

Search commands

If you want iBooks Author to do its search based on a text selection so that you don't have to enter the search text manually in the Find field, follow these steps:

1. **Select the text you want to search for.**

2. **Choose Edit⇨Find⇨Use Selection for Find.**

   Alternatively, you can press ⌘+E.

3. **Choose Edit⇨Find⇨Find to open the Find & Replace dialog box.**

   You can also open the dialog box by pressing ⌘+F.

   Your selected text appears in the Find field.

4. **Click Next to start the search.**

Even after you close the Find & Replace dialog box, you can still search for the last-specified search term: Press ⌘+G to find the next occurrence or Shift+⌘+G to find the previous occurrence. These keyboard shortcuts are like using the Next and Previous buttons in the Find & Replace dialog box, except you don't need that dialog box to be open.

When iBooks Author finds text, it selects that text in your book page, so you can see its context before committing to a replacement. (If you choose Replace All, you don't get to see the found text; iBooks Author just automatically changes every instance.) If the selected text isn't visible on the screen for some reason, choose Edit⇨Find⇨Jump to Selection or press ⌘+J to force iBooks Author to present that part of the book onscreen.

The Find & Replace dialog box also provides an Advanced pane that gives you more control over your search, as shown in Figure 3-7. (You can use the Simple pane, which appears by default, to get just the basic options.)

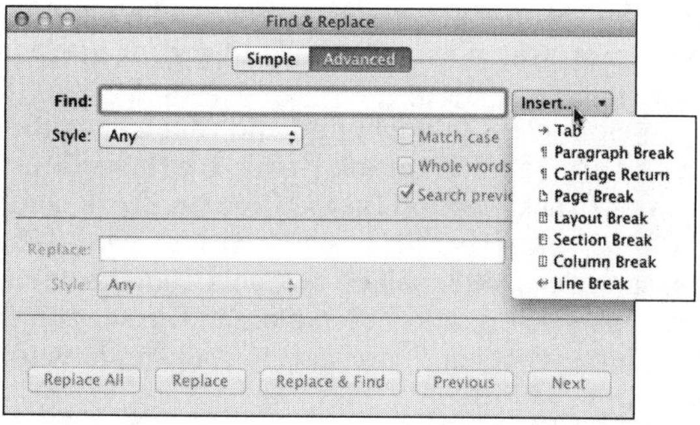

Figure 3-7: The Advanced pane of the Find & Replace dialog box.

Search constraints

The Find section of the Find & Replace dialog box's Advanced pane has three check boxes that let you constrain your search to the specified parameters:

- ✔ **Match Case:** If this option is selected, the search finds only text whose capitalization matches that in your Find field.

- ✔ **Whole Words:** If this option is selected, the search finds only whole-word versions of the text in your Find field. That means text that has a space both immediately before and immediately after it, begins a paragraph and is followed by a space or by punctuation, or text that has a space before it and punctuation immediately after it. Thus, if you search for *word* and have this option selected, iBooks Author ignores words that contain the text *word* but also have other text, such as *words, foreword, sword,* and *wordy.*

- ✔ **Search Previous Text (Loop):** If this option is selected (which it is by default), iBooks Author searches your entire book for the search term, starting at the current location, going to the end of the book, and looping back to the beginning of the book. If the option isn't selected, iBooks Author searches only from the current location to the end of the book.

Searching special characters

To search for special characters, such as page breaks and line breaks, choose an option from the Insert pop-up menu in the Find section of the Find & Replace dialog box's Advanced pane; likewise, choose an option from the Insert pop-up menu in the Replace section to include a special character in the replacement text. (Figure 3-7 shows the pop-up menu.) You can insert multiple special characters by choosing each in turn. An icon for each special character you chose appears in the Find and/or Replace fields.

The special characters you can find and replace via the Insert pop-up menu are Tab, Paragraph Break, Carriage Return, Page Break, Layout Break, Section Break, Column Break, and Line Break.

You can also search and replace symbols and special text characters, such as ¶, à, €, ¡, and ©. I explain in the section "Special characters and invisibles," later in this chapter, how to insert such characters and symbols.

Replacing styles

You can restrict the search to text with a specific character style or paragraph style applied by choosing an option from the Style pop-up menu in the Find section of the Advanced pane. All paragraph and character styles in your book appear in the pop-up menu's options. But you can't search for text that has a specific list style.

Likewise, you can apply a different style to the replaced text by choosing an option from the Style pop-up menu in the Replace section of the pane.

You can't use the Find & Replace dialog box to remove a character style from the searched text.

By default, the Style pop-up menus are set to Any, which means to ignore the text's style information. If you choose Any as the style for the search term, you can choose a specific style for the replacement term. That can come in handy if, for example, you want certain words, such as proper names, to always have a bold character style applied — such as to highlight car models' names in a book on cars. You would replace the name with itself, selecting the desired character style in the Replace section's Style pop-up menu.

The Style pop-up menus don't distinguish between character and paragraph styles, so you can easily accidentally replace text's character style with a paragraph style, which causes the entire paragraph to be restyled with the chosen paragraph style — rarely what you want.

Also, you can't search for all text by using a specific style and have iBooks Author apply a replacement style to it; you need to do that via the style drawer, as explained in the section "The style drawer," earlier in this chapter.

Proofreading your text

We all make mistakes, and the wide variety of English versions — with their differing spellings, grammars, and commonly accepted styles — means it's a challenge to maintain correctness and continuity in editorial projects. You can't automate such language correctness and continuity because some rules are ambiguous or contextual, but you can use software tools to help.

Don't count on these tools too much. They both miss errors and get some issues wrong. Think of them as a backup check for those times you got distracted or as a flag for what you should check yourself — and as an indication of where you may need to improve your own spelling and grammatical skills.

Grammar checking

iBooks Author provides a tool called Proofreader that combines capitalization and grammatical check in one tool, looking for both at the same time. Choose Edit➪Proofing➪Proofreader to open the Proofreading dialog box.

The Proofreading dialog box uses a very simple interface, as Figure 3-8 shows, that displays its suggestions in the Alternatives list box, provides a text field that initially displays the original text and in which you can enter what you want to replace the text with, gives an explanation of the detected issue, and displays your original text. After you make a selection or enter replacement text, click Correct to make the change and move on to the next issue. Of course, you can ignore the suggestion and leave the text alone by simply clicking Next. Like typical spell checkers, you move from one finding to the next, dealing with each in turn.

You also can have iBooks Author check for possible grammatical and style errors while you're working, without having to open the Proofreading dialog box:

✔ **One issue at a time:** Choose Edit➪Proofreading➪Proofread to have iBooks Author look for the nearest grammatical issue to your current text position and highlight the suspect text onscreen. I don't recommend using this option, though, because it's an ungainly menu sequence that has to be run each time you want to find the next issue and because you don't get any feedback about what the suspected issue is.

✔ **While you work:** Choose Edit➪Proofreading➪Proof as You Type. iBooks Author marks grammatically suspect text with a green dotted underline. Of course, that markup doesn't tell you what iBooks Author suspects is wrong with that text in the way that the Proofreading dialog box does, but the live proofreading option is very handy for catching typos and other simple errors while you type and edit.

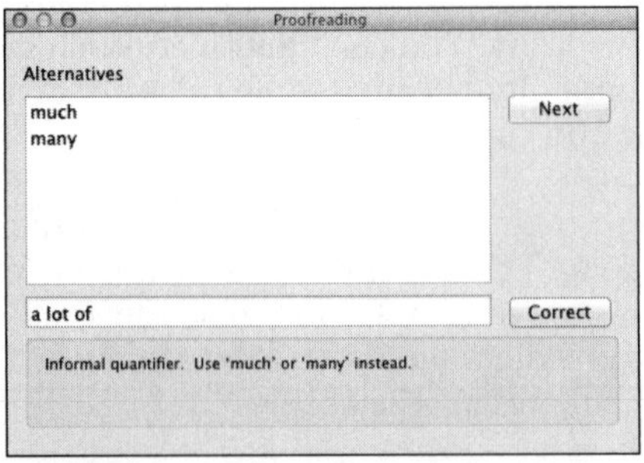

Figure 3-8: The Proofreading dialog box.

Regardless of whether you enable Proof as You Type to find issues while you write and edit, you can — and should — always use the Proofreading dialog box at the end of the project to deal with issues you were unsure of or didn't notice during the writing and editing process. And, of course, have an actual person proofread the book, as well, to handle the issues that the tool can't and to know which issues to ignore because iBooks Author identified them incorrectly.

Spell checking

By default, iBooks Author checks your spelling while you type or edit text. The red dotted lines beneath words indicate the suspected spelling errors. You can turn that feature off (or back on) by choosing Edit⇨Spelling⇨Check Spelling as You Type.

If you want to find the next possibly misspelled word in your document, choose Edit⇨Spelling⇨Check Spelling or press ⌘+; (semicolon); the next suspect word is highlighted. I don't recommend this option for the same reason I don't recommend using the similar grammar-checking tool described in the preceding section: It's too much work for each misspelling you want to find.

Instead, I recommend using the Spelling and Grammar dialog box, shown in Figure 3-9. You access this tool by choosing Edit⇨Spelling⇨Spelling or pressing Shift+⌘+; (semicolon). Despite the dialog box's title, it *doesn't* check grammar — only spelling.

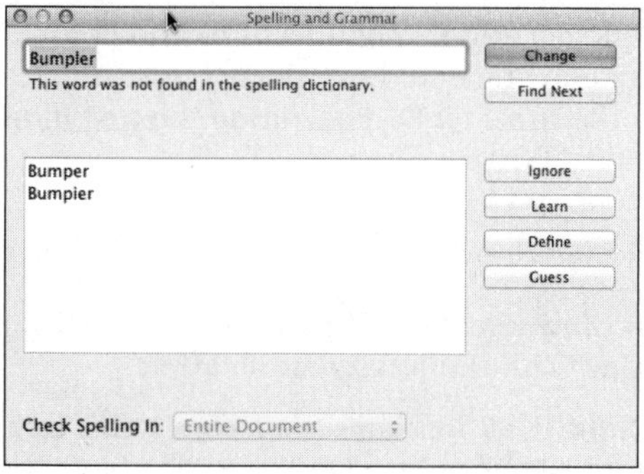

Figure 3-9: The Spelling and Grammar dialog box (which checks only spelling).

The spell checker is similar to those you find in other applications. The suspect word appears in the field at top, and suggested replacements are in the list below. Pick a replacement or modify the suspect word yourself; then click Change.

iBooks Author doesn't give you the option to replace all occurrences of the suspect word; you have to deal with each instance separately — a primitive approach compared to most other programs. This method can cause you to skip a change that you actually want to make because you're clicking away mindlessly on the umpteenth instance of the same issue.

The Spelling and Grammar dialog box gives you other options, too:

- ✔ **Ignore:** Leave the word as-is.
- ✔ **Learn:** Tell iBooks Author to consider the word correct.
- ✔ **Define:** If you're not sure if the word is real, click Define to open the Mac OS X Dictionary application.
- ✔ **Guess:** If you don't think the suggestions are right, click Guess to get more suggestions.

Finally, ignore the Check Spelling In pop-up menu; it's permanently unavailable because the spell checker always checks the entire document (excluding layouts). It's likely that at some point Apple will add options to this menu via an update to iBooks Author, such as Current Chapter or Current Selection, at which point the pop-up menu would become active.

Lookup

iBooks Author also provides tools to help you look up words and phrases, such as to verify their meaning or to find out more about them. For example, an editor might want to add context around a specialized term, and she could use these tools to discover that context. Access the tools by first selecting the text in question and then choosing Edit➪Writing Tools.

The options are

- ✔ **Look Up in Dictionary and Thesaurus:** Opens the term in the standard Mac OS X Dictionary application
- ✔ **Search in Spotlight:** Searches your Mac's files by using the Spotlight tool, which is Mac OS X's search facility
- ✔ **Search in Google:** Does a web search in your default browser
- ✔ **Search in Wikipedia:** Searches the Wikipedia online encyclopedia (www.wikipedia.com) in your default browser

Auto-correction

iBooks Author can correct common misspellings and capitalization errors while you type. You set this auto-correction in the

Preferences dialog box's Auto-Correction pane. To open the
Preferences dialog box, choose iBooks Author⇨Preferences or
press ⌘+, (comma), and then click the Auto-Correction icon button
to go to the Auto-Correction pane. The options are similar to those
in other word processors and desktop publishing applications:

- ✔ **Use Smart Quotes:** Replaces keyboard quotes (' and ") with
  their typographic equivalents (' '").

- ✔ **Fix Capitalization:** Corrects uncapitalized first words in
  sentences.

- ✔ **Superscript Numerical Suffixes:** Superscripts *st, nd,* and *rd*
  when they immediately follow a numeral, such as 32nd or 1st.

- ✔ **Automatically Detect Web and Email Addresses:** Adds live
  hyperlinks to these items (see Chapter 7).

- ✔ **Automatically Detect Lists:** Looks for paragraphs beginning
  with an asterisk (*) or a numeral, and then converts them into
  bulleted or numbered lists while you type.

- ✔ **Automatically Use Spell Checker Suggestions:** Corrects misspellings when you type them. Don't use this option in any
  book that has technical jargon, historical quotes, poetry, or
  vernacular because too much text that's legitimate for those
  contexts would be incorrectly replaced while you type.

- ✔ **Symbol and Text Substitutions:** Lets you add your own misspellings and other corrections, as well as any character
  sequences that you want automatically replaced with specific
  text or symbols (such as replacing *jws* with *John Wiley & Sons*
  or *(c)* with ©).

Special characters and invisibles

When you're writing and editing text, you use several invisible
characters, such as paragraph returns and spaces, that you may
want to see while you're working on a book because they help you
verify the text is correct. For example, displaying the symbols for
these characters onscreen lets you see that you really did use a
paragraph return rather than a line break to separate paragraphs.
It also lets you more easily find issues such as extra spaces or see
where the text includes forced page and column breaks (see the
section "Break and keep settings," earlier in this chapter).

To see these symbols, choose View⇨Show Invisibles or press
Shift+⌘+I; the same actions hide the invisibles. The light blue symbols for these characters (which don't appear when you print or

in the e-book viewed on the iPad) are the same as pretty much any editing software uses, such as the small dot for a space and ¶ for a paragraph break.

Many books — especially the textbooks that Apple has suggested iBooks Author be used to create — use special characters, from accented letters to special symbols. Mac OS X has a tool called the Character Viewer (shown in Figure 3-10) that lets you find and insert any of hundreds of such characters — called *glyphs* — available in your Mac's fonts. You can use the Character Viewer directly from iBooks Author by following these steps:

1. **Choose Edit⇨Special Characters.**

   The Character Viewer appears.

2. **Click an option in the list of glyph types at the left side of the Character Viewer to narrow down your choices.**

   Alternatively, you can search for a character based on a description of it in the Search field.

3. **Double-click a glyph to insert it at the current text location.**

4. **Click the Close box when done to close the Character Viewer.**

You can see a pane of recently used glyphs in the Character Viewer by clicking the Recently Used option at left and your favorite glyphs by clicking the Favorites option below Recently Used. To add glyphs to the Favorites list, select the glyph with a single click and then click the Add to Favorites button on the right.

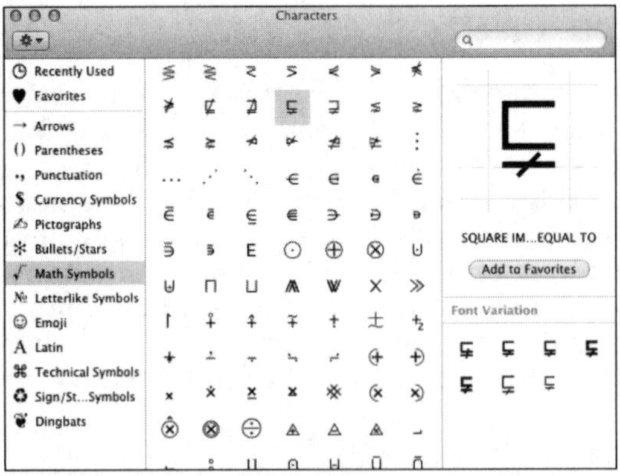

Figure 3-10: The Character Viewer.

You can also add special characters to your text by using their keyboard shortcuts. You can find these shortcuts visually by following these steps:

1. **Choose System Preferences to open the System Preferences application.**

2. **Click the Language & Text icon button.**

   The Language & Text system preference opens.

3. **Open the Language & Text system preference's Input Sources pane.**

4. **Select both the Keyboard & Character Viewer option and the Show Input Menu in Menu Bar option.**

5. **In Mac OS X menu bar, click the icon menu that displays an asterisk (*) in a box, and then choose its Show Keyboard Viewer menu option.**

   An onscreen keyboard opens.

6. **Hold down the Option key.**

   The Keyboard Viewer's display changes, showing all the characters you can get by pressing and holding Option when you click them. For example, the O key on the Keyboard Viewer changes to ø, indicating that pressing Option+O results in the ø character.

7. **Hold down Option+Shift and click a letter to have the Keyboard Viewer display the characters available when you hold Option+Shift and press a letter.**

   For example, pressing Option+Shift+O gets you Ø.

8. **To insert accents (the orange keys in the Keyboard Viewer), press the accent's shortcut, release the keys, and then click the letter you want to apply it to in your text.**

   For example, when you hold Option in the Keyboard Viewer, the E key turns to the ´ symbol (the acute accent) and its key turns orange. That means if you press Option+E, release the keys, and then press a vowel such as O, you get the acute accent on that vowel. For example, pressing Option+E, releasing the keys, and pressing O results in ó.

9. **When done, click the Keyboard Viewer's Close box to close it.**

The Mac's Help Center (which you can access by choosing Help from the Mac OS X menu bar in any application) lists the various ways to use special characters. Search for *accents* to get the related help topics.

Laying Out Text

In addition to working with the text itself, several layout-oriented actions affect how the text appears in the book. Some actions are design-oriented, such as adding colored backgrounds to sidebars or specifying text wrap, and I cover these actions in Chapter 4. But several actions affect the text itself, so I cover them in the following sections.

Setting columns, margins, and alignment

By default, your text boxes — including the layouts' text boxes for the mainbar — run the text across their width in one column, but you can change that setting in the Layout inspector's Layout pane. Just follow these steps:

1. **Open the Inspector by clicking the Inspector icon button in the toolbar.**

   Alternatively, you can choose View➪Show Inspector or press Option+⌘+I.

2. **Click the Layout icon button to go to the Layout inspector, and then open its Layout pane.**

3. **Enter the number of columns you want in the Columns text field.**

   Alternatively, you can use the stepper controls to change the number of columns.

4. **(Optional) Deselect the Equal Column Width option if you want columns' widths to differ.**

   You can set the desired column widths in Step 5.

5. **(Optional) Double-click the value in the Column column and enter a new value to change the column width if you don't like the default value.**

   If the Equal Column Width option is selected, changing any column's value changes all column values. If it's deselected, you need to change each column's width independently. Either way, if your columns' widths total more than the text box can accommodate, iBooks automatically sets the widths to the largest values that fit in the text box.

6. **(Optional) Double-click the value in the Gutter column and enter a new value if you don't like the default value.**

The gutter is the space between columns.

If the Equal Column Width option is selected, changing any gutter's value changes all gutter values. If it's deselected, you need to change each gutter's width independently. Like with column widths, iBooks Author overrides your gutter settings if they cause the columns to exceed the text box's width.

Figure 3-11 shows a two-column text, as well as the Layout inspector's Layout pane.

Figure 3-11 also shows the text in the second column aligned to the bottom of the text box. You can set that option in the Text inspector — not in the Layout inspector. Follow these steps to make text-box alignment changes:

1. **Open the Text inspector and go to its Text pane.**

The Text pane is also shown in Figure 3-11.

2. **Click the button in the top-right in the Color & Alignment section that corresponds to how you want to align the text.**

You can use these buttons to align the text to the top, center, or bottom of a text box.

If you have multiple-column text (as shown in Figure 3-11), iBooks Author doesn't distribute the text evenly across the columns, but instead fills each column until it runs out of text, and it then aligns the text in the partially filled column per the settings in the Inspector's Layout pane. That's rarely the layout effect you want, so for all practical purposes, use the alignment features only for single-column text boxes.

3. **Specify the Inset Margin control at the bottom of the Text pane.**

Use its slider, field, or stepper controls to create a margin between the text box boundary and the text, as shown in Figure 3-11. You usually add such a margin when you have a boundary line or a background color so that the text doesn't abut the line or the colored edge.

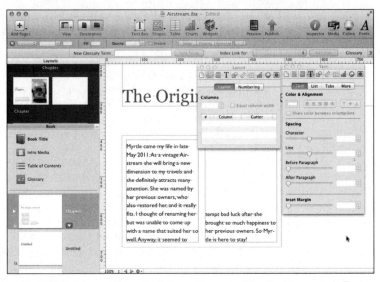

Figure 3-11: The Layout inspector's Layout pane and the Text inspector's Text pane for a multicolumn text box.

Flowing text

Text in your mainbar text box flows from page to page automatically. But what if you want to flow text among other text boxes, such as from the chapter opener to the next page?

Text flow limits and options

iBooks Author doesn't handle text flow in the same way that a traditional desktop publishing program does: You can't link existing text boxes however you want to specify the order in which text flows from text box to text box (that's what each link specifies). Instead, iBooks Author limits linking to certain text boxes on certain types of pages.

Here are the limits and possibilities:

✔ You can't link text between text boxes that you create.

✔ You can't link text from linkable text boxes to existing text boxes.

✔ You can't link text boxes in the layouts from one section to another, from one chapter to another, or between chapters and sections — all linked text boxes in a particular section or chapter layout can link only to text boxes in the same section or chapter layout. The same is true for book pages: You can link text boxes only across pages within the same section or chapter.

✔ The mainbar text boxes that are predefined in the layout for chapters, sections, and pages (see Chapter 2) are automatically linked to the text boxes in pages you create in the book from the layout templates.

✔ The text boxes in the first pages of chapter layouts and some section layouts don't have a linkable text box, so text from that first page can't flow to other text boxes. If you want text to flow from the first page of such layouts, you need to add a linkable text box to those pages and get rid of the original unlinkable text box if you no longer need it for other text.

By the way, you can tell whether the text boxes on first pages have more text than they can display — a + (plus sign) symbol appears in at the center of the text box's boundary when you select that text box.

✔ You can create new text boxes that link from these linkable text boxes, both in layouts and in book pages.

In other words, you need to start with the linkable text boxes that Apple provides in its templates' layouts. You can resize them, reformat them, and otherwise modify them, but you must not delete them if you want linkable text boxes.

If you select a linkable text box, an input indicator (a blue triangle in a box) appears at the upper-left of the text box's boundary, as shown in Figure 3-12. That triangle input indicator means that text box is the source for the text flow. An output indicator also appears at the bottom-right boundary. If that output indicator is a blue triangle in a box, the text box isn't linked to any further text boxes. (You can think of the input indicator as the From indicator and the output indicator as the To indicator.) If an indicator is a solid blue square, that means it's already linked to another text box, as I explain in the following section.

If you don't see those indicators, click the boundary itself. If you still don't see those indicators, your text box isn't linkable.

Linking a text box to a new text box

To link a linkable text box to another, follow these steps:

1. **Select a linkable text box.**

2. **To create a text box that precedes this text box in your text flow, click the input indicator at the upper-left of this text box.**

   Or if you want to create a text box that follows this text box in your text flow, click the output indicator at the bottom-right of this text box.

   The pointer gains a + (plus sign) symbol, as shown in Figure 3-12.

3. **Click anywhere outside the source text box to add a new text box.**

   The pointer displays an X while you hover over another text box, indicating you can't create a new text box there.

   If you created the new text box after clicking the input indi-cator of the source text box, the new text box is now the source for the text box whose input indicator you clicked, and the text now begins in that new text box and flows to the original text box.

   If you created the new text box after clicking the output indicator of the source text box, the new text box contains any overflow from the text box whose output indicator you clicked, and the text now flows into that new text box from the original text box.

4. **Format and position the new text box however you like — like any other text box.**

   You can click and drag the corner handles to resize the text box, drag the text box to move it, and format it by using the Inspector, as described in Chapter 4.

Figure 3-12: Click the input indicator for a text box to link to a new text box from which the text in the existing text box now flows.

Breaking and rerouting text flows

When you select a text box, you may see a solid input or output indicator, not the usual + (plus sign) icon in a box. That means the text box's text is already flowing elsewhere from this text box (if the output indicator icon is a solid blue square) or to this text box (if the input indicator icon is a solid blue square).

You can break the text flow from such a solid indicator, causing the text to stop flowing to the next text box in the flow (if you have selected the output indicator) or from the previous text box in the flow (if you have selected the input indicator). Just follow these steps:

1. **Select the solid indicator.**

2. **Hover the pointer over the linked text box's boundary.**

   The pointer displays an X symbol next to it to indicate that you're about to break the link.

3. **Click the boundary of the text box.**

To reroute the text flow, follow these steps:

1. **Select the solid indicator.**

2. **Hover the pointer somewhere other than over a text box.**

   The pointer displays a + (plus sign) symbol next to it to indicate that you're about to create a new text box in the text flow.

3. **Click outside any existing text box to add a new linked text box.**

If the text originally flowed to another text box, the text now flows to the new text box and then from there to the other text box. Essentially, you're adding another link in the flow of text, with each linkable text box being a link in that chain.

Figure 3-13 shows such a chain of linked text boxes. The indicators within the flow are solid blue squares; and the input indicator for the first text box in the flow and the output indicator for the last text box in the flow both appear as the icons of a blue triangle in a box.

The lines shown in Figure 3-13 between the output and input indicators show the text flow when you're viewing a layout. Unfortunately, you don't get these flow lines when working in the book's actual pages.

In Figure 3-13, the input indicator is in the bottom text box and the output indicator is in the top text box, so here the text flows from the bottom text box to the middle text box, and then on to the top text box. Typically, you don't flow text that way, so be sure to arrange the linked text boxes in a sensible order in your layout (not like in Figure 3-13!).

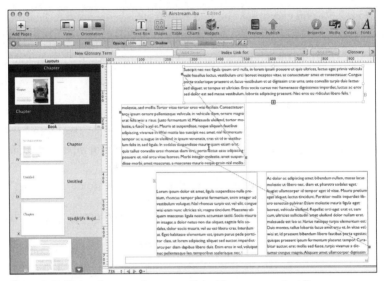

Figure 3-13: These three text boxes are linked in a common text flow.

When you're working in book pages, the overflow indicator appears, shown at the bottom of the topmost text box in Figure 3-13. This indicator looks like a + (plus sign) in a black-framed square and lets you know that the flow contains more text than can fit in the text boxes. In other words, your text is cut off. You can create another text box by using the output indicator for that text to flow into, whether on this page or another in the section or chapter. Or you can edit the text to fit. That's up to you!

Chapter 4

Adding and Formatting Objects

* *

In This Chapter

▶ Putting objects in your iBooks Author e-book

▶ Formatting and laying out your objects

▶ Working with images

▶ Using an object's formatting as a default style

* *

*W*ith your templates set up and your text set (as I describe in Chapters 2 and 3, respectively), the typical next step is to add the graphical objects to your book — and in iBooks Author, any dynamic objects you may have, as well, such as videos and presentations. Of course, you might also add placeholders for some of these objects to your layouts.

iBooks Author's landscape orientation is designed to show objects in your e-book, and you can specify their exact placement on the page. But, as Chapter 2 explains, portrait orientation hides many floating and anchored objects in your layout; these objects that include captions (see Chapter 5) are retained but shrunk to preview icons and placed in the thumbnail track of the vertical layout. Inline objects are retained in the mainbar text when in portrait orientation. (Chapter 2 explains floating, anchored, and inline objects.)

Adding Objects

As noted in Chapter 2, the basic process for adding objects is simple. If you add a text box, table, or widget by using either of the following methods, you can later add the contents to the place-holder object iBooks Author creates for you (the placeholder has a gray background with an icon for the content type):

- ✔ In the toolbar, click the appropriate icon button or icon menu for the object you want to create. You can choose from the Text Box and Table icon buttons and from the Shapes, Charts, and Widgets icon menus. (When you click the Shapes, Charts, or Widgets icon menus, a pop-up menu appears with the various types available for that object).

- ✔ From the Insert menu, choose Text Box, Table, or an option from the Shape, Chart, or Widget submenus, depending on what type of object you want to add.

When you add an object by using the following methods, the object created contains the selected file's contents:

- ✔ Choose Insert⇨Choose or press Shift+⌘+V to open a settings sheet where you can select a compatible file from your Mac or any storage device connected to it, then click Insert.

- ✔ For some widgets, you can drag a compatible file from a folder or the desktop through Mac OS X's Finder and drop it onto your layout or page. (I list the compatible file formats in the following sections.)

Figure 4-1 shows a placeholder object for an image gallery widget, into which I'm dragging an image. If you add a chart, you can enter its data immediately, or else use the sample chart data provided until you later add the actual data. If you add a shape, the actual shape is added to the layout. (Chapter 5 covers creating and editing tables and charts, as well as how to use shapes to create illustrations.)

Text files

By choosing Insert⇨Chapter from Pages or Word Document, you can import Microsoft Word .doc and .docx files and Apple Pages files. As Chapter 3 explains, doing so creates a new chapter in the e-book. You can't drag such files into your layout, but you can drag in RTF (Rich Text Format) files and any text-only files (.txt, .html, and so on); they are added in their own text boxes.

You can copy and paste text from any application by using the copy and paste commands (see Chapter 3). You can also control whether formatting is copied along with the text (see Chapter 2).

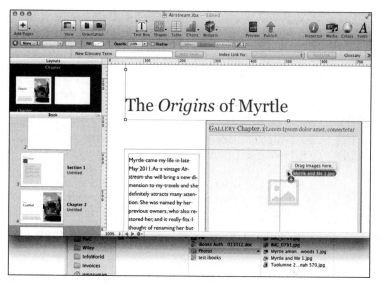

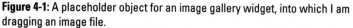

Figure 4-1: A placeholder object for an image gallery widget, into which I am dragging an image file.

Graphics files

There are several ways to bring graphics — photos, screenshots, drawings, charts, and original artwork — into your iBooks Author book:

- ✔ **Bitmap images:** Import or drag in most popular bitmap formats (used for photos, screenshots, and other images composed of pixels) — GIF, JPEG, Photoshop (`.psd`), PICT, PNG, RAW, TIFF, and Windows bitmap (`.bmp`).

- ✔ **Photos:** Use the Media Browser panel's Photos pane to access bitmap images (usually photos) stored in the iPhoto application that comes preinstalled on new Macs. (I explain how to use the Media Browser in the section "Video, screencast, and audio files," later in this chapter.)

- ✔ **Vector graphics:** You can also import or drag in two vector formats (typically used for drawings): Adobe Illustrator (`.ai`) and PDF (for multipage PDF files, only the first page is visible in the e-book).

- ✔ **3D graphics:** You can import or drag in Collada 3D graphics (`.dae`) files into your layout. If you import 3D objects that are too complex to appear on the iPad, a blank preview image appears in the iBooks Author layout — that means your e-book's readers can't see the 3D image, either.

✔ **Other graphics:** Copy and paste graphics from other applications as their own objects, including charts created in Excel and Numbers, though these graphics are pasted as static graphics, without their accompanying data.

Graphics files brought into iBooks Author by using these methods are typically placed in the book document as their own objects, with two exceptions:

✔ You can drag or paste an image into an interactive image object (note that you can't import images into it via menus or the Inspector).

✔ You can drag any of the supported image formats into an image gallery, as well as add images to it by choosing Format➪Gallery➪Add Image. (Chapter 6 explains both image galleries and interactive objects.)

Any graphics in imported Word and Pages files are retained and treated as inline objects in your text flow. But graphics in pasted or dragged-in text aren't retained.

Spreadsheet files

You can't import, or drag and drop, Microsoft Excel or Apple Number spreadsheets into an iBooks Author file, but you can paste their data into an iBooks Author chart. If you paste all or part of a spreadsheet into a chart, as described in Chapter 5, iBooks Author creates or modifies a chart from that data. If you copy a spreadsheet or part of it into a layout or page (rather than into a chart object), it's pasted as a table in iBooks Author.

Tables

You can import tables that are part of a Word or Pages file when you create a new chapter based on that document file. These tables are treated as inline objects in your text flow.

Although you can paste Excel or Numbers spreadsheets as tables or into charts, tables copied from other applications into layouts or pages, or included in dragged-in files, are converted to text, losing their tabular formatting. Table data copied from other applications into charts is retained, but iBooks Author doesn't recognize axis labels as it does for pasted Excel and Numbers data.

Presentation files

You can drag and drop Apple Keynote presentation files (.key) or a Keynote file exported to HTML (drag the entire folder onto the widget) into an iBooks Author file. But you can't drag and drop files that are in the Microsoft PowerPoint format. Fortunately, if you own Keynote for Mac OS X or iOS, you can use it to open PowerPoint files and convert those files to Keynote format, then drag and drop the converted files into iBooks Author.

In iBooks Author versions prior to 1.1, the Choose button to select a Keynote file (which you can find in the Widget inspector's Interaction pane) doesn't work. It does work in iBooks Author 1.1 and later, though.

Chapter 6 explains how to work with Keynote presentations.

Video, screencast, and audio files

You can add iPad-compatible MPEG-4 video (.m4v) files — including movies and screencasts — and AAC audio (.m4a or .m4v) files.

But you can't use the usual import or drag-and-drop methods. Instead, you need to drag and drop a file from the Media Browser panel — from its Movie pane for video files and its Audio pane for audio files — onto a page or layout, or onto a placeholder widget (which is labeled Movie, even though it also supports audio files). To open the Media Browser, click the Media icon in the toolbar or choose View⇨Show Media Browser; these actions also close it. Figure 4-2 shows a media object and the Media Browser.

You can't import QuickTime (.mov) videos or MP3 audio files into iBooks Author, so you need to convert them to a compatible format to use them. Also, copy-protected media files don't import, even if they're in a supported format.

To be available for import into iBooks Author, the media files must be in the content libraries of iTunes (for video and audio), iMovie (for video), iPhoto (for images), or GarageBand (for audio), or they must be in the Mac's Movies folder (for video). You can't import files from other locations.

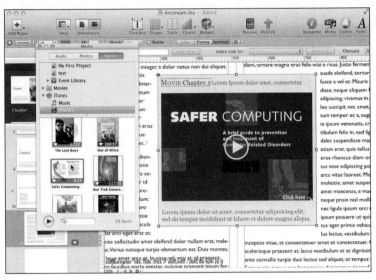

Figure 4-2: The Media Browser lets you add a video file to a media object.

But it's easy to get media files into iMovie and iTunes:

✔ In Mac OS X's QuickTime Player application, open the audio or video file, and then choose Share➪iTunes or Share➪iMovie to export a video file to iTunes or iMovie. This export also converts incompatible formats to those compatible with iBooks Author.

✔ Use video-conversion applications such as HandBrake (www. handbrake.fr) to convert video files to a compatible format, then move them into the Movies folder on your Mac.

✔ Add audio files to iTunes by choosing File➪Add to Library or pressing ⌘+O. If the file isn't in the AAC format, convert it to AAC by selecting it in iTunes and then choosing Advanced➪Create AAC Version.

By the way, the QuickTime Player application that comes with all Macs also lets you record what's occurring on your screen — these videos are called *screencasts* — so you can show people how to work with software or how other aspects of Mac OS X work. If you run Windows in a desktop virtualization environment, such as Parallels Desktop (www.parallels.com) or VMware Fusion (www. vmware.com), you can also capture Windows how-to's on your Mac. Ambrosia Software's Snapz Pro X (www.ambrosiasw.com) also records screencasts, in addition to taking screenshots with more controls than Mac OS X's Grabber utility provides. Also, you can find more-professional paid screencast programs, such as Camtasia (www.techsmith.com), for both Mac OS X and Windows, whose video files you can convert to an iBooks Author–compatible format in QuickTime Player like you would any video file.

HTML snippets

You can add web widgets — a type of interactive application that uses the web's formatting language — by entering the HTML code yourself. You can also import, or drag and drop, a web snippet (.wdgt) created by Apple's Dashcode utility into iBooks Author, as explained in Chapter 6.

Formatting Objects

You can apply several attributes to objects to give them a more visual style: background color, borders, transparency, curved corners, and drop shadows.

If you use any of Apple's iWork applications — Pages, Keynote, or Numbers — the formatting controls and Inspector should be familiar because iBooks Author uses the same techniques.

Working with colors

You can apply colors to objects' backgrounds and boundaries, as well as to text. But how do you get those colors? You use the Colors panel, which you open by clicking the Colors icon button in the toolbar, choosing View➪Show Colors, or pressing Shift+⌘+C; the same commands hide it. The Colors panel has several panes that you can use to access a variety of *color models* (ways of defining and naming colors): the Color Wheel, Color Sliders, Color Palettes, Image Palettes, Crayons, and RCWeb panes. Figure 4-3 shows four of the panes.

Defining colors

To define a color, go to any of the Color panel's panes. All the panes have one common feature: The Sampler tool (the magnifying glass icon). Click it, then move the Sampler tool to an object in your layout that has the color you want to add. For example, you might hover the Sampler tool over a specific location in a photograph to sample its color. Click where you want the color to be sampled and note how the color now appears at the top of the pane. That color is now the active color, meaning you can apply it to an object in the layout or save it for later use.

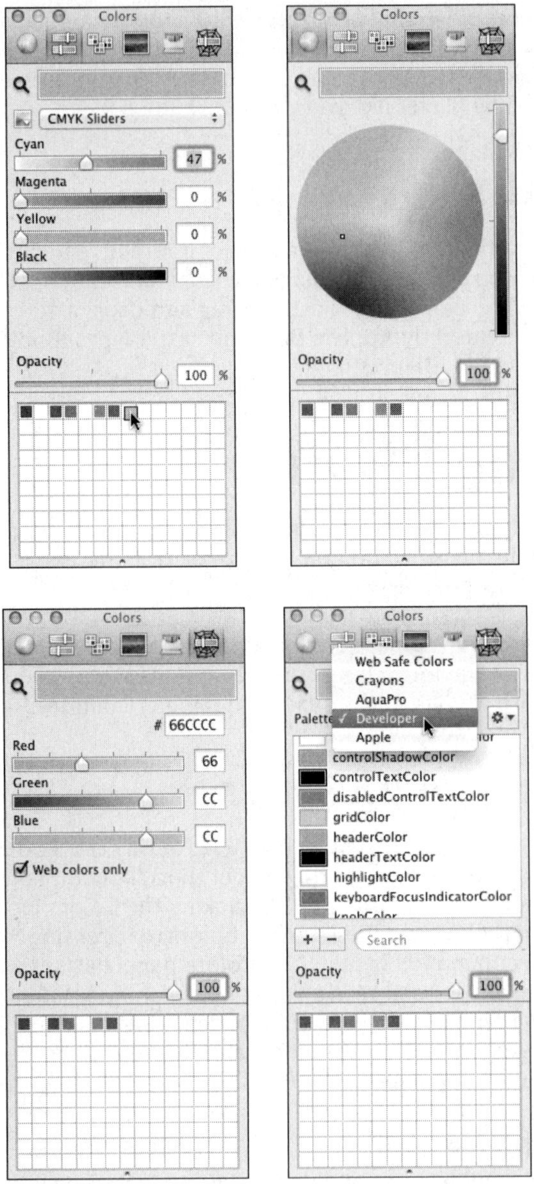

Figure 4-3: The Colors panel's Color Sliders, Color Palettes, Color Wheel, and RCWeb panes.

To save the active color, simply click and hold that color, drag the cursor onto a blank square at the bottom of the pane, and then release the mouse button. That square now has the color applied, and you can click that square at any time to make that color active.

Otherwise, the panes work differently:

✔ **Color Wheel:** Drag the square on the color wheel to make the active color the desired color. Increase or decrease the color's brightness by using the slider at left.

✔ **Color Sliders:** Choose the desired color model (CMYK, RGB, LAB, or Gray Scale) from the unnamed pop-up menu below the Sampler tool, and then use the sliders to mix the desired color to create a new active color. The CMYK color model is meant for print reproduction, so use the RGB or LAB color models for creating your e-book's colors because those color models are optimized for onscreen display. Use the Opacity slider to lighten the color you mixed; 100-percent opacity means you get the full color, 0 percent you means it's transparent.

To the left of the pop-up menu, where you choose your color model, an icon menu (a square multicolor swatch) also appears, from which you can choose the specific color calibration for the current color model. For e-books, this icon menu is irrelevant, so you can ignore it. Apple uses the Colors panel in other applications, some of which are intended for professional reproduction on printing presses and other methods; for some of these reproduction methods, calibrating the color to the methods' specific capabilities improves color fidelity. But in an e-book, that's unnecessary.

✔ **Color Palettes:** Choose an existing set of colors (called a *palette*) from the Palette pop-up menu to make it the active color. A set of individual colors (called *swatches*) appears. The Developer and AquaPro palettes contain the colors and shades used by Mac and iOS developers for user-interface elements, and are meant to be used for objects designed to look like controls (such as buttons). Here are some of the actions you can take in the Color Palettes pane:

  • *Adjust the opacity of a swatch.* Use the Opacity slider. Using this slider doesn't change the swatch itself, it changes the active color. Drag the active color to an empty color square to save that altered swatch for later use.

  • *Create your own palette.* Choose New from the Action icon menu (which looks like a gear). To name the palette, choose Rename from the Action icon menu.

  • *Create a swatch.* Use the Sampler tool, the color squares, or any of the other panes to create a new active color, and then (in the Color Palettes pane) click the + (plus sign) icon button to create a swatch from that color.

- *Rename a swatch.* Double-click a swatch's name, and when the name becomes an editable field, type in the new name.

- *Delete a swatch.* Select a swatch and click the – (minus sign) icon button.

The + (plus sign) and – (minus sign) icon buttons work only for a palette you created.

✔ **Image Palettes:** By default, this pane has just one palette available — Spectrum, which shows a color spectrum. But you can add your own image palettes by using one of two methods:

- In the unnamed pop-up menu below the color area, choose New from File. (The unnamed pop-up menu is set to Palette by default.) In the New Color Palette dialog box that appears, select a graphic, and click Open; iBooks Author adds that graphic to the Image pop-up menu and displays a preview of it in the color area below the Image pop-up menu.

- Add an image that you've copied from elsewhere, such as from a graphic in your e-book or from Photoshop, and then choose New from Clipboard from the unnamed pop-up menu to copy that image into the Image Palettes pane.

When you choose an image by using either method, it appears in the color area, and you can then click in that image thumbnail to select a color from it as the active color.

To duplicate a palette in the pane, choose that palette in the Image pop-up menu. Then, in the unnamed pop-up menu, choose Copy⇨New from Clipboard to create an unnamed palette from that copied palette.

Name or rename the current palette by choosing Rename from the unnamed pop-up menu. Delete the current palette by choosing Remove from the unnamed pop-up menu.

✔ **Crayons:** Choose a crayon to make its color active. You can use the Opacity slider to change its level of transparency.

✔ **RCWeb:** You can specify a color by using the standard HTML color-definition method in a couple of ways:

- *Color value:* If you know it, enter the six-digit color value in the text field preceded by the # character to create the desired active color, such as FF0000 for pure red. The first pair of digits defines the level of red, the second pair defines the level of green, and the third pair defines the level of blue. 00 means no color, FF means full color. Each digit is hexadecimal, meaning there are 16 levels: 0 to 9 for the first ten levels, then A to F for the next six levels.

- *Sliders:* Adjust the sliders to create the active color. Select the Web Colors Only check box to restrict the slider to the colors that reproduce well on any browser.

Because iBooks Author e-books are designed for use on the web, you don't need to restrict yourself to the common web colors.

Regardless of the method you use to define the color in the RCWeb pane, you can adjust the opacity of the color by using the Opacity slider.

Applying colors to text

To apply color to text, follow these steps:

1. **Select the text.**

2. **Open the Colors panel by clicking the Colors icon button in the toolbar.**

   Or you can choose View➪Show Colors or press Shift+⌘+C.

3. **Define or choose a color from the panel, as described in the preceding section.**

Alternatively, you can apply color through the Inspector by following these steps:

1. **Click the Inspector button in the toolbar.**

   Or you can choose View➪Show Inspector or press Option+⌘+I.

   The Inspector opens.

2. **Click the Text pane to open the Text inspector.**

3. **Click the Text label to open the Text inspector's Text pane (shown in Figure 4-4).**

4. **Open the Colors panel by clicking the color swatch.**

5. **Define or choose a color from the color swatch, as described in the preceding section.**

The Text inspector's Text pane lets you select whether the color applied to the text is retained in both page view orientations. If the Share Color Between Orientations option in the Text pane is selected, the applied text color appears in both landscape and portrait orientations. If it's deselected, the color is visible only in the orientation in which it was created; the other orientation has either the original color or a color you apply separately when working in that orientation. (This option doesn't work in versions of iBooks Author prior to 1.1.)

Figure 4-4: In the Text inspector's Text pane, you can apply color to text selections.

Applying colors to objects

It's slightly more complicated to apply colors to objects than to text (explained in the preceding section). Follow these steps:

1. **Select the object to color.**

   Note that for charts, you can apply colors to the chart object's container or to its bars and other data-derived portions. To apply colors to the data elements, select an element, rather than the entire chart; all elements based on that same row series have the color applied. (See Chapter 5 for discussion of row series.)

2. **Click the Inspector button in the toolbar.**

   Alternatively, you can choose View➪Show Inspector or press Option+⌘+I.

   The Inspector opens.

3. **Go to the Graphic inspector, shown in Figure 4-5, by clicking its icon button at the top of the Inspector.**

You can apply color to three attributes: background (the fill), border (the stroke or line), and the drop shadow. After you open the Graphic inspector, you can apply colors to the fill, stroke, and/or drop shadow (explained in the "Drop shadows" section, later in this chapter).

To color a fill, follow these steps:

1. **Choose Color Fill from the Graphic inspector's Fill pop-up menu.**

2. **Click the color swatch below the pop-up menu.**

   If the Colors panel isn't already open, it appears (and stays open until you close it).

3. **Select a color from the Colors panel, as described in the preceding section.**

   Whatever you set as the active color is applied to the fill. You can also drag the active color or a color square onto the Fill swatch in the Graphic pane to apply that color.

Figure 4-5: The Graphic inspector lets you apply color to an object's fill, line, and/or drop shadow, as well as transparency to the entire object.

To color a stroke, follow these steps:

1. **In the Graphic inspector, choose Line from the Stroke pop-up menu.**

2. **Specify a color for that stroke by clicking the color swatch below the menu and selecting a color from the Colors panel.**

   If the Colors panel isn't already open, it appears when you click the color swatch (and stays open until you close it).

To color a drop shadow, follow these steps:

1. **In the Graphic inspector, be sure the Shadow check box is selected.**

2. **Click the color swatch below the option and select a color from the Colors panel.**

To remove a color from any of these elements, you need to remove the fill, stroke, or drop shadow itself. To remove a fill, choose None from the Fill pop-up menu in the Graphic pane. To remove a stroke, choose None from the Stroke pop-up menu. To remove a drop shadow, deselect the Shadow option.

Applying colors to tables

You use a similar method to apply colors to the components of a table as you use to apply colors to objects (see the preceding section). Select a table, or one or more cells of a table, and then click the Table inspector's Table pane, as shown in Figure 4-6. Three swatches open the Colors panel for you to apply the desired color to the desired table element: Cell Borders, Cell Background, and Row Color (this swatch has no label in the Table pane).

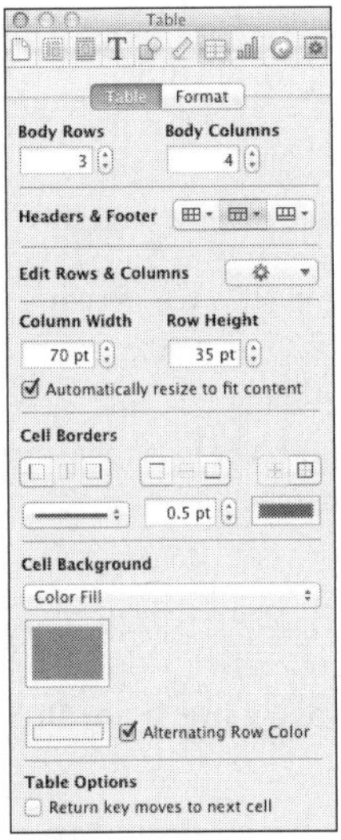

Figure 4-6: In the Table inspector's Table pane, you can apply colors to strokes, cells, and rows.

If you select a table object, the color chosen in the Cell Border swatch applies to the entire table's cell borders. If you select specific cells, the cell border applies to just those cells; also, the Cell Background pop-up menu becomes active, from which you can choose Color Fill to display the swatch you click to open the Colors panel so that you can specify a color.

You can also apply color to specific outside, row, and column borders. Click the desired border (the pointer changes to a pair of triangles), and then use the Cell Border swatch to apply a color to it. You may need to double-click a border to select it — clicking it once makes the table the active object, and the second click selects the specific border.

No matter whether you select the entire table or specific cells, you apply a color fill to rows by using the swatch to the left of the Alternating Row Color option at the bottom of the Table pane. You must select the Alternating Row Color option if you want to apply a color. As the name implies, the selected color applies to every other row. The rows to which the color isn't applied are white, and you can't change these rows' color (such as by applying a background color to the table in the Graphic inspector) like you can with most other objects.

Setting object attributes

The Graphic inspector lets you set three common object attributes: background fills, borders, and drop shadows. You can set these attributes for objects, such as images, text boxes, charts, tables, widgets, and shapes.

Select the desired object, and then go to the Graphic inspector to apply the desired attributes. In the case of a chart, you can apply these attributes both to the object's container and separately to each data element (more precisely, to all data elements based on the same data row). Figure 4-7 shows an example in which all three attributes are in use; in this case, in a chart.

Figure 4-7: A chart with an image background, and a color fill, borders, and drop shadow for the chart elements.

Background fills

Select an object, then choose one of the options from the Fill pop-up menu. Here are the menu choices:

✔ **None:** Remove any fill; the default for newly created objects.

✔ **Color Fill:** Apply a color to the object's background, as described in the preceding section.

✔ **Gradient Fill:** Apply a *gradient,* a transition from one color to another. Figure 4-8 shows an example. The top swatch sets the From color, and the bottom swatch sets the To color. You can reverse these colors by clicking the Swap icon button (the curved double arrow) to the right of the swatches. Use the Angle wheel or field to set the direction of the gradient; click the right-pointing arrow button to set the angle to 0° (left to right) and the down-pointing arrow button to set the angle to 270° (top to bottom).

✔ **Image Fill:** Place an image as the background, as shown in Figure 4-7 (the Airstream photo behind the bars). Follow these steps:

   1. **Choose this option for a specific object.**

      The Open dialog box appears.

   2. **Select the desired image and click Open to insert it.**

      The Graphic pane changes to show an image preview for that image fill, as well as add the Choose button and an unnamed pop-up menu that controls how the image appears.

You can change that image later by clicking the Choose button to select a new image via the Open dialog box, or by dragging an image from the Finder onto the thumbnail preview.

You control how the image appears by using the unnamed pop-up menu; its options are

   • *Tile:* Repeats the image at original size as many as times as needed to fit the background.

   • *Original Size:* Displays the image at its actual size. If the image is too small, it's centered in the object. If the image is too large, the excess portion is cut off.

   • *Stretch:* Enlarges or reduces the image to fit the object. This option distorts the image if its proportions differ from the object's proportions.

- *Scale to Fit:* Enlarges or reduces the image to fit the object, while maintaining the original image's proportion. If necessary, this option cuts off *(crops)* the image from the top, bottom, and/or sides.

- *Scale to Fill:* Works like Scale to Fit, but cuts off more of the image so that what appears is more magnified in size.

✔ **Tinted Image Fill:** Works like Image Fill, except that it adds a swatch that you can click to open the Colors panel and apply an overlay tint to the image. By setting the color's opacity with the Color panel's Opacity slider (see the "Defining colors" section, earlier in this chapter), you determine how strong the tint is.

The only object you can't apply a fill to is a straight line shape.

If you apply a fill to a curved line, the fill appears below the curve and ends at an imaginary line between the two endpoints.

If you're working with text, you can set a background for the current text selection or paragraph by using the Text inspector's More pane. In the Background Fills section, select the Character option to apply a color to the selected text, and/or deselect the Paragraph option to apply a color to the current paragraph. Use corresponding swatches to set the background colors. (Chapter 2 explains text formatting in depth.)

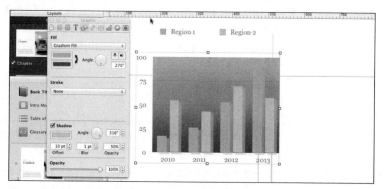

Figure 4-8: A gradient background and its settings in the Graphic inspector.

Strokes

A *stroke* is a line, whether a border around an object, a border around a table cell or chart element, or an actual line. As shown in Figure 4-7, the Graphic inspector's controls for strokes are simple. Just follow these steps:

1. **In the Graphic inspector, choose Line in the Stroke pop-up menu to apply a border to the selected object or element.**

   If you don't choose Line, none of the following options are available.

   If you choose an object, as opposed to a line or data element in a chart or a line, that has a caption applied (see Chapter 5), you get an additional border outline option in the Stroke pop-up menu: Picture Frame. As Figure 4-9 shows, choosing this option applies a graphic around the object, with a choice of 12 frame graphics. Use the Scale slider to determine how large the frame is.

2. **Choose the type of stroke that you want to use from the unnamed pop-up menu below the Stroke pop-up menu.**

   By default, this pop-up menu shows a straight, thin line. The other options are a dotted line, a dashed line, a thick line with angled endpoints, and three kinds of crayon-like lines.

3. **Click the swatch to open the Colors panel, and then select a color for the stroke, as described in the "Applying colors to objects" section, earlier in this chapter.**

4. **Set the stroke's thickness by entering a value in the Weight field.**

   Or you can use the stepper controls to adjust the current value.

5. **If you created a line by using the Shapes options (see Chapter 5), choose the ending style for each end of the line from the two Endpoints pop-up menus.**

   These menus offer ten options, such as arrowheads.

   Endpoint options aren't available for object borders, just line shapes.

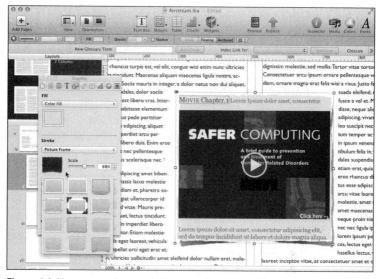
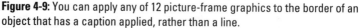

Figure 4-9: You can apply any of 12 picture-frame graphics to the border of an object that has a caption applied, rather than a line.

You can also apply strokes to table elements in the Table inspector and to text paragraphs in the Text inspector (not via the Graphic pane, as for objects):

- ✔ **Tables:** If you're working with a table, you can set the stroke weight and color for a border, row line, column line, or cell border by using the controls in the Cell Borders section of the Table inspector's Table pane, shown in Figure 4-6. You can set the stroke's type, color, and size, as well as which sides of a cell or table have strokes using the various buttons in the Cell Borders section. (If you use spreadsheet software, these controls are similar to those in Excel and the same as used in Numbers.)

- ✔ **Text:** If you're working with text, you can set a border for the current paragraphs using the Text inspector's More pane. In the Borders & Rules pop-up menu, choose the desired line type, then use the adjacent swatch to set its color and the adjacent field and stepper controls to set the stroke weight. Use the icon buttons below to determine where the border appears for the paragraph, and use the Offset field or stepper controls to determine how far from the text the border appears. (Chapter 2 explains text formatting in depth.)

Corners

When you select an object with a border, note the blue circle icon near the upper-left corner. That handle lets you set the curvature of the object's corners. Drag it to the right to increase the curvature and drag it to the left to reduce the curvature. Figure 4-10 shows an object with a curved corner.

If your curve cuts into the contents of the object, you can create an internal margin for that object's contents to compensate. To add a margin, follow these steps:

1. **Open the Widget inspector.**

   Click the rightmost icon button in the Inspector to get the Widget inspector.

2. **Go to the Layout pane by clicking its label in the Widget inspector.**

3. **Select the Background check box.**

4. **Use the Background option's slider, field, or stepper controls to increase the margin so that the contents fit within the curved corners.**

   Chapter 5 explains how to use captions with objects and how to use the other settings in the Widget inspector.

Figure 4-10: By sliding the blue circle handle, you can increase the corners' curvature, as shown at right.

Drop shadows

The Graphic inspector also contains controls for *drop shadows,* simulated shadow that gives the object the illusion of floating above the other contents around it. Select the Shadow check box to add a drop shadow to an object; Figure 4-7 shows a drop shadow applied to a chart's bars.

If you apply a drop shadow to an object that has no fill, the shadow applies to its border (if it has one) and to its text. Figure 4-11 shows a drop shadow applied to such a text box; it also shows the controls for shadows.

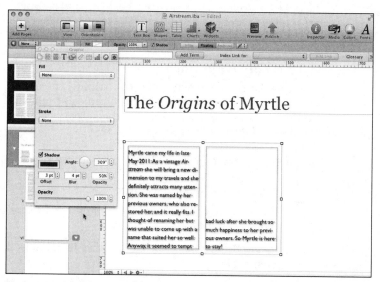

Figure 4-11: Applying a drop shadow to a text box that has no fill causes the shadows to appear in the text.

You can apply these options to your drop shadow:

- ✓ **Color:** Click the color swatch to open the Colors panel, and then make a selection.

- ✓ **Direction:** Use the Angle wheel, its field, or its stepper controls. An angle of 0° has the drop shadow appear to the right of the object or text.

- ✓ **Distance from the object:** Use the Offset field or stepper controls.

- ✓ **Sharpness:** Use the Blur field or stepper controls; larger values enlarge the drop shadow's size but also blur the shadow until it looks like a glow, rather than a shadow.

- ✓ **Transparency:** Use the Opacity field or stepper controls; the default is 50 percent.

Be careful not to use the Opacity slider, field, or stepper controls at the bottom of the inspector's Graphic pane; that sets the transparency for the entire object.

Opacity

In the "Apply color to objects" section, earlier in this chapter, I explain how to use the Opacity slider in the Colors panel to control the degree of transparency applied to a color. The Graphic inspector also has an Opacity slider, field, and stepper controls (at the bottom of the inspector). These controls specify the level of transparency — but for the entire selected object.

Accessibility information

You can also set an invisible object attribute: the object's accessibility information.The visually impaired can enable this attribute on the iPad to have the contents of the screen read aloud by using the iPad's VoiceOver capability.

To enter the text to be read aloud, follow these steps:

1. **Open the Widget inspector.**

   Click the rightmost icon button in the Inspector to get the Widget inspector.

2. **Go to the Layout pane by clicking its label in the Widget inspector.**

3. **Click in the Accessibility Description field, and enter the text.**

Applying Image Masks and Enhancements

When working with *bitmapped images* (that is, all supported images except for Adobe Illustrator and PDF files), you can also apply a variety of enhancements and effects. For all images, you can also apply what's called an alpha filter to make portions of the image translucent. Also, for all images, you can *mask* (cut out, or crop) portions of the image.

Enhancing bitmapped images

To apply image enhancements or effects — similar to the basic photo-retouching capabilities in Apple's iPhoto, Apple's Aperture, or Adobe's Photoshop Elements — follow these steps:

1. **Choose View⇨Show Adjust Image to open the Adjust Image panel, shown in Figure 4-12.**

2. **Select an image.**

3a. Apply enhancements and effects by using the appropriate sliders in the Adjust Image panel.

You can change brightness, contrast, saturation, color temperature, color tint, sharpness, light exposure, and color levels. While you make the adjustments, they're applied live to your image.

3b. Click the Enhance button to have iBooks Author try to figure out the best enhancements to apply.

If you click Enhance, any enhancements you've applied through the sliders are replaced with iBooks Author's choices.

To undo any applied enhancements, click the Reset Image button.

4. When done, choose View⊃Hide Adjust Image to hide the panel.

Alternatively, click the panel's Close box.

Figure 4-12: The Adjust Image panel.

Using the Instant Alpha feature

In professional image editors, such as Adobe Photoshop and Apple Aperture, you can create alpha *channels* (image regions) that let you change the transparency for the image colors in those channels.

iBooks Author makes this complex capability extremely simple. Just follow these steps:

1. **Choose Format⇨Image⇨Instant Alpha.**

2. **Click and hold in the portion of the image that you want to make translucent.**

   The image must be a bitmap format, as described in the "Graphics" section, earlier in this chapter.

3. **Drag the pointer.**

   The further you drag, the more of the image whose colors are in the same range as the initially clicked area is selected.

4. **Release the pointer.**

   Voilà! The selected image areas are translucent.

5. **Repeat Steps 2 through 4 to use the Instant Alpha tool to make other portions of the image translucent.**

   For example, follow these steps for portions of the image that have different color ranges.

6. **Press Return when you're done.**

To restore the original image, select the image and then choose Format⇨Remove Instant Alpha.

Figure 4-13 shows the Instant Alpha tool in use.

Figure 4-13: The Instant Alpha tool highlights the selection in magenta (left) and creates a translucent sky (right).

Masking images

A *mask* is a crop; both terms mean to cut out unwanted portions of an image. Most programs let you crop an image by choosing its selection handles (sometimes you need to choose a cropping tool first) and move those handles into the image. Whatever appears outside the selection frame when you release the handles is cropped out.

But iBooks Author doesn't work that way: If you pull in a selection handle for a selected image, iBooks Author resizes that image.

To crop an image in iBooks Author, you use the masking tool by following these steps:

1. **Select an image.**

2. **Choose Format⟹Image Mask.**

   Alternatively, press Shift+⌘+M.

   The masking controls appear, as shown in Figure 4-14:

   - *Move the selection handles.* Determine the size of the image to keep by dragging the mask's selection handles to the desired positions. The shape and size of the image are determined by these handles' positions.

   - *Drag the image.* Drag an image within its mask to determine what portion of the image is retained. Positioning the selection handles usually accomplishes this goal, but you can refine the portions displayed or change it altogether by dragging the image.

   - *Use the slider.* Adjust the position of the slider to make the image larger or smaller within the mask.

   You use these controls to determine what portion of the image appears in the e-book (and in iBooks Author) and in what shape and size.

3. **Click Edit Mask to apply the masking.**

   The masking tool doesn't disappear, so you can still change the size of the image, but you can't adjust its selection handles (they now scale the image) or drag the image within the mask to change what portion is shown. To make those changes, repeat Step 2.

4. **To undo your masking, select the image and choose Format⟹Unmask.**

   Or press Shift+⌘+M.

Figure 4-14: An image being masked.

You can also apply nonrectangular masks to an image. Choose Image➪Mask with Shape, and then choose one of the 12 options from the submenu. These masks work like the standard rectangular shape, which happens to be the first option in the submenu.

Laying Out Objects

After you get your elements in your layouts and pages (as described in Chapter 2), chances are that you want to adjust their size and position to work well in your page layout's design. You may also want to distribute multiple objects evenly, and perhaps flip or rotate them. You likely want text to wrap around overlapping objects so that the text doesn't overlap those other objects, even when they overlap its text box.

Before I explain how to work with objects in the layout (see the following sections), I need to note some issues with selecting objects in iBooks Author. Like with all other Mac programs, you click anywhere in an object to select it, which causes the object's boundary and selection handles to appear. But it can be difficult to select an object in iBooks Author, especially if an overlapping object is already selected. If you can't select an object, try the following:

✔ Click its boundary. (Choose View➪Show Layout Boundaries or press Shift+⌘+L to show all objects' boundaries, not just the currently selected object's boundary.)

✔ Click outside all objects, such as in the outer margins of a page, and then try clicking the object again.

✔ Move an overlapping object out of the way, and then try clicking the desired object. (You can put the other object back later.)

✔ Move an overlapping object below the desired object by selecting that in-the-way object and then choosing Format➪Arrange➪Send to Back or pressing Shift+⌘+B. But I've found moving an object below the one you want to select often doesn't help in selecting the desired object like it does in most other programs.

Sizing and positioning objects

The process for resizing objects should be familiar because iBooks Author uses the same method that practically every other program uses: When you select an object, eight selection handles appear, one on each corner and one midway along each side. You drag the handles to resize and reshape the object based on where you move the various handles.

Like in most programs, when you reshape or resize text boxes or tables, the text size for the contents are unaffected. The contents of other objects are scaled to fit within the objects' new shape, which may cause different margins on the sides than on the top and bottom. Any outside boundary's stroke weight and any drop shadow's size are also unchanged, but effects such as shadows in a picture frame can also be distorted based on the new shape. Figure 4-15 shows an example.

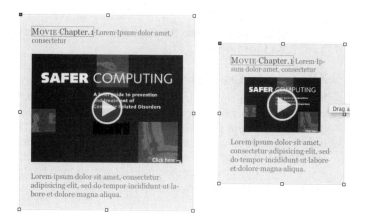

Figure 4-15: When an object (left) is resized (right), its text size doesn't change, but other elements are resized and may have their margins adjusted.

To move an object, click and drag it to the new location. If you're selecting a text box or table, you might have trouble dragging the object if iBooks Author selects the text inside the object and assumes you're trying to expand that text selection. In that case, clicking and dragging from the boundary usually lets you move the object.

Alignment and size indicators

When you drag an object or resize it, alignment and size indicators appear, as shown in Figure 4-16. When iBooks Author detects that one or more of your boundaries is close to that of another object, it displays these indicators so that you can ensure proper alignment with nearby objects, if that's your goal.

You can turn these indicators off, if you prefer, by following these steps:

1. **Choose iBooks Author⇨Preferences.**

   Or press ⌘+, (comma).

   The Preferences dialog box opens to the General pane. (Click the General icon button to go to it if you're working in another pane.)

2. **In the General pane, select the Show Size and Position When Moving Objects check box.**

3. **(Optional) Click the Rulers icon button to open the Rulers pane, and then specify the display options for these indicators.**

   You also set the ruler increments' values, alignment guides' colors and positions relative to objects, and object size and position indicators' color and values in the Rulers pane.

4. **When done, close the Preferences dialog box by clicking its Close box.**

Aligning multiple objects

If you select multiple objects, iBooks Author can align them for you. Choose Format⇨Arrange Objects, and then choose the desired alignment from the submenu, which contains the options Left, Center, Right, Top, Middle, or Bottom. All objects are aligned with the object furthest in the direction you select. For example, if you choose Left, all selected objects are aligned to the leftmost object in the group.

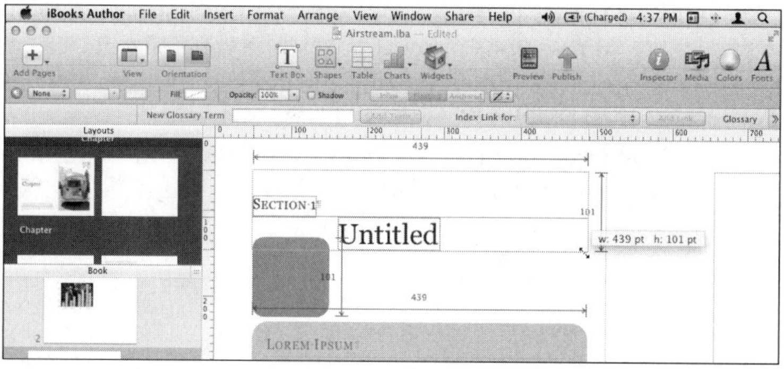

Figure 4-16: These visual indicators can help you align selected objects with other objects.

Distributing multiple objects evenly

Also, if you select multiple objects, you can have iBooks Author distribute them evenly: Choose Format⇨Distribute Objects⇨Horizontally (or Vertically, depending on how you want to distribute them).

If the objects are already spaced so that they don't overlap in the direction in which you're distributing them, the objects are kept within the area they currently occupy and spaced evenly within that area. But if the objects overlap in the direction in which you're distributing them, iBooks Author moves them so that they don't overlap; instead, it has them abut each other along the chosen direction, which enlarges the area the group occupies.

Specifying size and position

You can precisely specify the size and position of a selected object by using the Metrics inspector, shown in Figure 4-17:

- ✔ **Width and Height:** Enter values in these fields or use the stepper controls to change their values.

- ✔ **X and Y:** Enter values in these fields or use the stepper controls to change their values.

By default, the X and Y coordinates start at the upper-left of the page (meaning the 0,0 point is the upper-left corner of the page), but you can make that point the center of the page by going to the Preference dialog box's Rulers pane and selecting the Place Origin at Center of Ruler check box.

✓ **Constrain Proportions:** Select this option to keep the object's dimensions proportional while you resize it. This option is selected by default for images and widgets, and it's deselected by default for other objects.

✓ **Original Size:** For images only, select this option to restore the object to its original size.

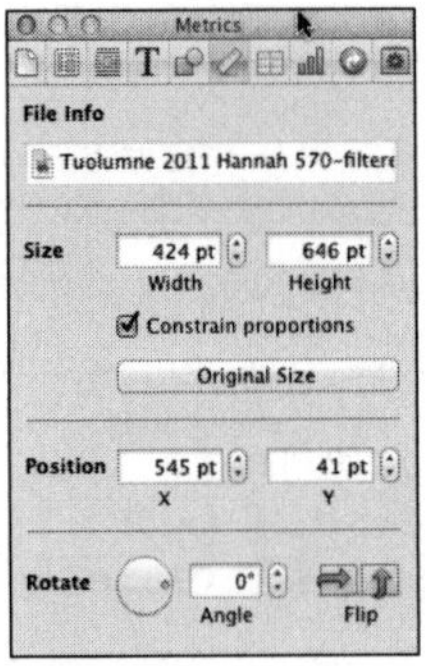

Figure 4-17: The Metrics inspector.

Stacking order

You can control objects' appearance by adjusting what's called their stacking order. When objects overlap each other, their *stacking order* determines how they overlap and thus what parts are visible — much like if you laid a series of cards on top of each other. (You can think of stacking as positioning objects relative to each other in the third — or *z* — dimension, whereas positioning them on the page addresses the *x* and *y* dimensions.)

By default, the stacking order is determined by when an object was created or added; later objects are above earlier objects in the stacking order and obscure those earlier objects where they overlap. But you can change the stacking order by selecting an object and using the following commands:

✓ **Move to the top of the stacking order.** Choose Arrange➪Bring to Front or press Shift+⌘+F.

✓ **Move up one level.** Choose Arrange➪Bring Forward or press Option+Shift+⌘+F.

✓ **Move to the bottom of the stacking order.** Choose Arrange➪Send to Back or press Shift+⌘+B.

✓ **Move down one level.** Choose Arrange➪Send Backward or press Option+Shift+⌘+B.

Flipping and rotating objects

You can apply the flip and rotation controls in the Metrics pane to text boxes, images, shapes, charts, and tables:

- ✔ **To flip an object:** Click the Horizontal Flip and/or the Vertical Flip icon buttons in the Metrics pane, or choose Arrange➪Flip Horizontally and/or Arrange➪Flip Vertically.

- ✔ **To rotate an object:** Select an object and click and drag within the Rotate wheel, enter a value in the Angle field, or use the Angle stepper controls to rotate the selected objects around their centers.

A more direct — but less precise — way to rotate an object is to select it (so that its selection handles appear), hold the ⌘ key, and then click and drag any of its selection handles to rotate the object around its center (it doesn't matter which selection handle you use). The pointer changes to a curved double arrow, indicating that rotation is enabled.

Grouping and locking objects

Often, when you have multiple related objects, you want to group them together so that you can move them as one object and prevent an individual element from being accidentally moved or resized. Grouping objects also lets you apply various commands and formatting to all the objects at the same time.

To create a group, select the objects you want in it, and then choose Arrange➪Group or press Option+⌘+G. To ungroup an object group, select the group, and then choose Arrange➪Ungroup or press Option+Shift+⌘+G.

Selecting multiple objects is the same in iBooks Author as in any Mac program. Click and drag to create a marquee rectangle around the objects you want to select, and then release the pointer. All objects within the marquee are selected; to select just specific objects instead, click the first object and Shift-click each additional object you want to select.

Also as in any Mac program, to remove an object from a group, you must ungroup the objects, and then select just those objects you want in the group.

You may also want to lock objects so that you can't accidentally alter them. To do so, select an object and choose Arrange➪Lock or press ⌘+L. iBooks Author disables all sizing, positioning, and formatting actions on locked objects. To unlock an object, select it and choose Arrange➪Unlock or press Option+⌘+L.

Setting text wrap

When you have objects intruding into text, you usually want the text to flow around those objects, which is called *text wrap*. To set text to wrap around an object, you use the Wrap inspector (accessed by clicking the third icon button from the left in the Inspector, which looks like a square in a sea of text). Figure 4-18 shows the Wrap pane and its settings for an example text wrap.

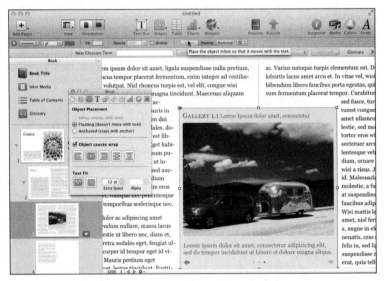

Figure 4-18: Specifying settings for a text wrap in the Wrap pane.

The controls are simple:

✔ **Object Causes Wrap check box:** Select this check box to enable text wrap around the selected object. Inline objects don't have this option available because they're treated like text characters (see Chapter 2 for more on inline objects and Chapter 3 for more on text settings).

✔ **Wrap Style icon buttons:** Select the desired wrap style from the five icon buttons. Each button shows how that style wraps text, as you can see in Figure 4-18.

✔ **Text Fit icon buttons:** Select the type of wrap by clicking the appropriate icon button, shown in Figure 4-18. The Square Wrap icon button (the first button) wraps the text around the object's boundary in a square; the Contour Wrap icon button (the second button) wraps around the visible contours of the object, such as a curved shape (see Chapter 5) or an image masked with a triangle shape (see the section "Masking images," earlier in this chapter), rather than the object's boundary.

✔ **Extra Space field and stepper controls:** Adjust the text distance from the object by entering a value in the field or by using the stepper controls to adjust its value.

The Wrap inspector also includes the Alpha control, which lets you make the text flow into areas of an image that you made transparent by using the Instant Alpha tool, described in the section "Using the Instant Alpha feature," earlier in this chapter. Follow these steps:

1. **Select the image to which you applied the Instant Alpha tool.**

2. **Select the Contour Wrap icon button (the second Text Fit icon button) if it isn't already selected.**

3. **Use the Alpha field or its stepper controls to reduce the value.**

   A value of 0% allows the maximum amount of text to intrude into the transparent image area, and a value of 100% allows no text to intrude (the same as having clicked the Square Wrap icon button).

The Alpha control doesn't work well. If you have an extremely simple image, such as a yellow circle on a red background, and use the Instant Alpha tool to make the red transparent, it works. But I couldn't get text to intrude into transparent areas of the various photos to which I applied the Instant Alpha tool, such as to remove the sky and have the text flow into that now-transparent part of the image.

Setting Default Object Styles

After you format your objects, you might wonder whether you have to re-create the same formatting for similar objects. Well, you don't.

Of course, if you format an object in a layout, all pages that use that layout have the same formatting. But that setup doesn't help you format similar objects in other layouts, nor those created on pages.

But you can tell iBooks Author to take the formatting of a specific object and apply it to all new objects of that same type. For example, if you have a specific style for your charts that you want to make the default, you can specify that iBooks Author automatically apply the formatting of one chart to all new charts. You can do the same for all text boxes.

Here's how to work with defaults:

✔ **Set a default style.** To set an object's formatting as the default style for that kind of object, select that object, and then choose Format➪Define Default Style for *Object Type*. From that point, each new object of that type that you create gets the selected object's formatting. Of course, you can modify the formatting of any object you create, as needed; the default style becomes the starting point for each new object of that type, not a straitjacket.

If you later change that original object's formatting, new objects you create continue to get the formatting saved as the default for that object type when you chose Format➪Define Default Style for *Object Type*. In other words, the object you created the default style from isn't used as a master in which subsequent changes are automatically used to update the default style.

✔ **Apply the default style.** You can reapply the default style to objects that either didn't have it applied or that you changed; select the object and choose Format➪Reapply Defaults to *Object Type*.

✔ **Update the default style.** If you want to update the default style, select any object of the same type that has the new or updated formatting and choose Format➪Define Default Style for *Object Type*. Existing objects aren't updated (you have to choose Format➪Reapply Defaults to *Object Type* to update existing objects' style individually).

Chapter 5

Working with Infographics

*I*f you've read Chapter 4, you know how to add objects to your e-book and format them. But there's more to objects than placing and formatting them. You use objects to convey meaning to the reader, and iBooks Author provides several capabilities to shape the presentation of that meaning.

That's what this chapter is all about: working on the presentation of information in infographics (charts, tables, diagrams, and so on that convey information). Often, such elements are called figures by publishers. The terms can be used interchangeably, but there is a subtle difference: An *infographic* is meant to tell a self-contained story, using a combination of text and graphics (a visual sidebar, if you will), whereas a *figure* can be any visual element used to illustrate or reinforce a point in the text.

Chapter 6 covers the controls over interactive objects that can also convey meaning in an iBooks Author e-book. For those objects, you do most of the content work in whatever program you used to create them, whereas with infographics, you do most of the content work within iBooks Author.

You also convey information through *sidebars,* text boxes that contain text related to the chapter's current topic but that isn't core to the topic. Sidebars are text boxes like any other, so you can check out the techniques for working with text in Chapter 3 and the techniques for formatting sidebars (you do want them to be visually distinct from the main text, after all) in Chapter 4.

Adding Object Captions and Titles

A fundamental aspect of objects in iBooks Author is the caption and its associated title. A *caption* is the text that describes an object, to give readers context for its content. Because the reference to a figure or other object in text can be separated from where the figure actually appears, a caption is useful to remind the reader of the figure's relevance to the topic at hand.

A *title* is the label for the caption. iBooks Author automatically numbers objects with captions in the order they appear. For example, if you have two images with captions in Chapter 3, iBooks Author labels them Image 3.1 and Image 3.2, and if you also have a table with a caption in the same chapter, iBooks Author labels it Table 3.1. As Chapter 7 explains, you can insert cross-references to figures in your text that iBooks Author uses to keep the in-text reference updated to the current label. In other words, while your figure labels are renumbered when you move, delete, and add them, the references to them in the text are kept up to date.

Many programs treat captions as independent text boxes that you then group with an image to keep them together. You can do that in iBooks Author, but you don't need to. And there's a strong reason you shouldn't: Only floating and anchored objects that have a caption applied are visible to the e-book's readers in portrait orientation. (Chapter 2 explains floating, anchored, and inline objects.)

Adding a caption and, optionally, caption title is easy. Just follow these steps:

1. **Select the object.**

2. **To open the Inspector, click the Inspector icon button in the toolbar.**

   Alternatively, you can choose View⇨Show Inspector or press Option+⌘+I.

3. **Click the Widget icon button (the rightmost one at the top of the Inspector) to open the Widget inspector.**

4. **If the Widget inspector's Layout pane isn't visible, click the Layout label to switch to it.**

5. **Select the Caption option to create a caption for the object.**

6. **(Optional) Select the Title option if you want to give the caption a title.**

7. **Double-click the placeholder caption to select it, and then type in (or paste) your own caption.**

8. **(Optional) If you enabled a title for the object, double-click the placeholder title to select it, and then type in (or paste) your own title.**

   Figure 5-1 shows an image with a caption and title applied, as well as the Widget inspector's Layout pane.

Adding captions and titles is even easier for widgets: iBooks Author automatically applies a caption and title to all widgets when you add them, whether it's a movie (video and audio), image gallery, Keynote presentation, interactive image, 3D image, review, or HTML snippet. It doesn't apply captions and titles automatically to charts, tables, shapes, or images, but you can apply captions to these elements, as needed, by following the preceding steps.

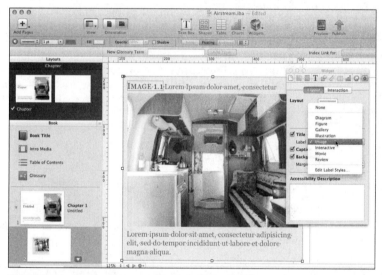

Figure 5-1: An image with a caption and title applied (center) and the Widget inspector's Layout pane (right).

As you can see in Figure 5-1, you have several options in the Widget inspector's Layout pane when working with captions and titles:

✔ **Label pop-up menu:** Change the label used in the title. Your options are None, Diagram, Figure, Gallery, Illustration, Image, Interactive, Movie, and Review. Choosing the Edit Label Styles menu option opens the Edit Label Styles settings sheet, shown in Figure 5-2, where you can

   • Add your own labels by using the + (plus sign) icon button.

   • Delete labels by using the – (minus sign) icon button.

- Change the numbering used for titles' numbers by using the Label Format pop-up menu.

- Apply a character style to the title by using the Character Style pop-up menu.

✔ **Background option:** Place a colored background behind the object, its caption, and its title. Select this option to display the background. It's gray by default, but you can change the color by using the techniques described in Chapter 4. Adjust the Margin slider to specify the margin between the object's boundary and its contents; the default is 10 points.

✔ **Layout icon menu:** Rearrange the layout of the object's elements. You can change the placement of the object's title, caption, and contents by choosing a different arrangement from the Layout icon menu, shown in Figure 5-2. In all arrangements, you can drag the image, movie, or other non-text content within the object to change its relative position and spacing; the object boundary adjusts automatically. If you choose the Freeform menu option, you can move the contents, caption, and title, not just the contents. If you choose the Banner menu option, you can move the contents and the combined caption and title, not just the contents.

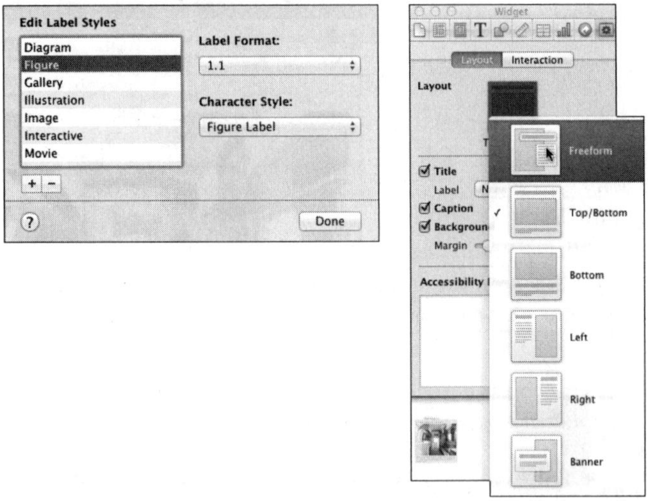

Figure 5-2: The settings sheet where you set title options (left) and the icon menu where you set a figure's layout arrangement (right).

You can set one more option for figures in the Interactive pane of the Widget inspector: the Full-Screen Only option, shown in Figure 5-3. Selecting this option has two effects:

✔ The contents appear in full screen on the iPad when tapped by the reader.

✔ The size of the object is reduced in iBooks Author to a preview size that the reader will see in iBooks before tapping the object. You can change that preview size by dragging the object's selection handles; click the Edit Frame button when you finish.

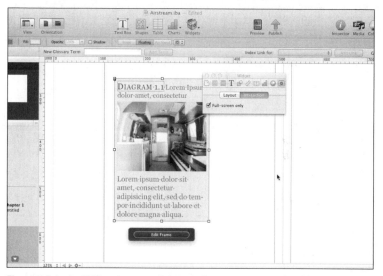

Figure 5-3: In the Widget inspector's Interactive pane, you can force objects' contents to appear in full-screen size on the iPad when a reader taps the preview image.

As Chapter 4 explains, after you set these options for an object, you can make that formatting the default style for all future objects of this type — so you don't have to remember your settings for each caption and title you create.

Creating, Editing, and Formatting Charts

A popular way of showing information visually is by using a chart, which converts series of data (such as sales over multiple financial quarters) into bars, lines, and other graphical presentations. iBooks Author lets you create such charts based on data, in much the same way that Microsoft Excel and Apple Numbers do.

To create a chart, use the Charts icon menu in the toolbar to choose the desired chart type (there are 19 types). Or you can choose Insert⇨Chart and then choose the desired chart type from the submenu that appears. iBooks Author creates a chart that uses sample data. It also displays the Chart inspector and the Chart Data Editor panel, all shown in Figure 5-4.

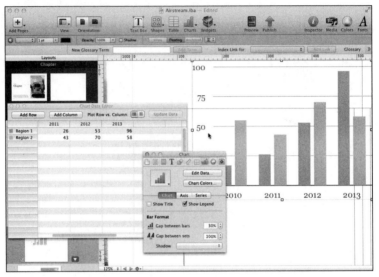

Figure 5-4: A new chart object, the Chart Data Editor panel, and the Chart inspector.

Working with data

In the Chart Data Editor panel, you can edit the data that powers your chart. In addition to accessing it from the Chart inspector, you can also choose Format⇨Chart⇨Show Data Editor or press Shift+⌘+D. Its controls are simple:

- ✔ Double-click a cell to edit its contents. (Cells can contain only numbers — no letters, symbols, or formulas.) Double-click an axis label (the topmost row and the leftmost column that have the gray backgrounds) to edit that label.

- ✔ Click Add Row to add data rows to the chart. Likewise, click Add Column to add data columns to the chart.

- ✔ Click either of the Plot Row vs. Column icon buttons to determine whether the row or column data (each column or row is called a *data series*) appears in the chart as the visual data. Colored squares appear next to the axis labels (called the *legend*). For example, in Figure 5-4, the Region data in each row is plotted against the column data range shown in the *y* axis, so those rows' values constitute the bars rising up into the *y* axis and resting on the *x* axis. (That is, the row data is used to create the visual data.) The legend's colored squares also let you know which bars, lines, and so on belong to which data series.

Rather than enter the data manually, you can paste Excel or Numbers spreadsheet data into a chart by following these steps:

1. **Select the data in Excel or Numbers that you want to paste into iBooks Author.**

2. **Choose Edit⇨Copy to copy that data.**

   Alternatively, you can press ⌘+C.

3. **In iBooks Author, select the upper-left cell in the Chart Data Editor panel for the selected chart.**

4. **Paste the data by choosing Edit⇨Paste.**

   Or you can press ⌘+V.

   iBooks Author detects the axis labels if you have them in that pasted data, and it adds rows and columns as needed to hold the pasted data.

 You can also paste table data from other applications, such as Word and Pages, but iBooks Author doesn't recognize axis labels in such data as it does for pasted Excel and Numbers data.

Formatting charts

You can apply a caption and title to a chart, as described in the section "Adding Object Captions and Titles," earlier in this chapter. But you can do much more formatting than that for a chart by using the Chart inspector. All charts have a set of common chart options at the top of the Chart inspector.

For most chart presentation types, the Chart inspector has three panes — Chart, Axis, and Series — that each have one or more sections. (Figure 5-5 shows the three panes.) The Chart inspector for pie charts has no panes, but it does present several pie-specific sections.

If you select the graphical portion of the chart, rather than the chart object, you can set its formatting as the default for all future charts of that type by choosing Format⇨Advanced⇨Make Default Style for *Chart Type* Type, and you can apply that saved format to a chart's graphical portion by choosing Format⇨Reapply Defaults to Chart.

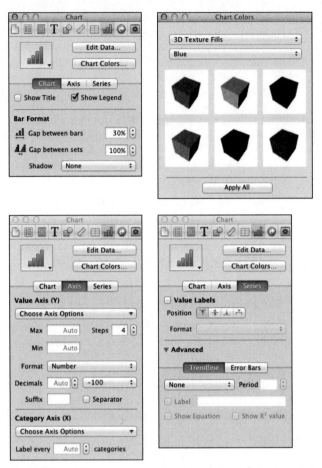

Figure 5-5: The Chart inspector's Chart pane, Chart Colors panel, Axis pane, and Series pane for a bar chart.

All charts

As shown in Figure 5-5, at the top of the Chart inspector are options always available, no matter which pane or other sections are active:

> ✔ **Presentation Type icon menu:** You can change the type of graphics used to present your chart data by selecting a different option from the Presentation Type icon menu's 19 options, which cover a range of bar, line, area, pie, scatterplot, and bar-and-line presentation types. The right side of the icon menu's options are 3D types. If you choose one of these types, the 3D Chart panel appears. Drag your pointer within that panel to change the rotation of the 3D chart, as desired.

(E-book readers can't change the chart rotation on the iPad, by the way, like they can with the 3D graphics covered in Chapter 6.)

✔ **Edit Data button:** Click the Edit Data button to open the Chart Data Editor panel, where you can edit the chart data, as explained in the preceding section.

✔ **Chart Colors button:** Apply the desired fill colors and textures to the chart's bars, lines, and pie segments by clicking the Chart Colors button, which opens the Chart Colors panel shown in Figure 5-5. In that panel, choose from the top pop-up menu the type of predefined fill you want (the options are 3D Texture Fills, 2D Image Fills, and 2D Color Fills). Then choose the desired predefined color scheme from the pop-up menu below (which has 12 options). Drag the preview swatch onto the chart element to which you want to apply that style; all elements in its data series get that fill and color scheme. Or click Apply All to apply the fill and color scheme to all the chart's data elements; iBooks Author determines the specific color for each data series' elements from the chosen color scheme's palette.

Bar charts

The options in the Chart pane, shown in Figure 5-5, control the display of the basic chart elements:

✔ **Show Title:** Select this option to add a title to the chart. The word Title appears above the chart, and you can edit it, as desired, by double-clicking it and entering (or pasting) your text.

✔ **Show Legend:** This option is selected by default and displays a legend for your chart, comprised of colored squares or circles (depending on the chart's presentation type) and the labels for which axis they represent. The legend appears in its own text box, and you can reposition it on the page or layout, as desired, by dragging it. If you don't want a legend to appear, deselect this option.

✔ **Bar Format:** If you're displaying the data in one of the eight bar formats or one of the two bar-and-line formats, this section appears in the pane. It includes three controls:

  • *Gap between Bars:* Set the distance between bars by entering a value in the field or adjusting its stepper controls.

  • *Gap between Sets:* Set the distance between bar groups by entering a value in the field or using its stepper controls.

  • *Shadow:* Specify an (optional) drop shadow for the whole group or just the selected bar by choosing an option from the pop-up menu.

The options in the Axis pane, shown in Figure 5-5, control the labels and formatting of the chart's *x* and *y* axes:

✔ **Value Axis (Y):** This pop-up menu has several sets of options that determine how the *y* axis appears. Unlike most pop-up menus in iBooks Author, you can choose multiple options in this menu; after you choose each one, a check mark appears to the left of its name. Here are the sets of options available:

- *Axis display:* These options control how the *y* axis appears. Show Axis shows the *y* axis's line. Show Chart Borders places a visible border around the entire chart data, with the left border being the *y* axis. Show Title places placeholder text for the *y* axis's title along its axis; double-click that text to edit it.

- *Axis labels:* These options control how the *y* axis's labels and values appear. Show Value Labels shows the numeric value for each increment along the *y* axis. For example, if your data starts at 30 and goes to 500, the chart may show for increments (of 125, 250, 375, and 500) along the *y* axis. Show Minimum Value displays the smallest data value in the chart at the bottom of the *y* axis (30, in this example).

- *Scale:* These options determine how the *y* axis's values increment; the options are Linear Scale, which provides even increments between the smallest value and the largest, and Log Scale, which uses an exponential logarithm to scale the increments; for example, if most data is in the range of 30 to 150 but one item has a value of 1,000, the chart reduces the space on the *y* axis between increments while the values increase, so the differences among the smaller values are more readily apparent and the distance to the largest value is shortened.

- *Tick marks:* These options determine where the tick marks appear relative to the *y* axis; these major tick marks show where the numeric increments fall for the selected scale. The options are No Tick Marks, Major Tick Marks Inside, Major Tick Marks Centered, and Major Tick Marks Outside. If you choose Show Minor Tick Marks, iBooks Author also displays interim indicators between the *y* axis's major tick marks to help the reader better calculate the value of bars or lines based on their height, using the additional tick marks as a guide.

- *Gridlines:* These options determine which lines appear across the chart to indicate the numeric values as an aid to the reader for visually assessing a bar's value. You can choose from two options: Show Major Gridlines places lines at the same locations as the major tick marks, and Show Minor Gridlines places lines at the same locations as the minor tick marks.

✔ **Scale values:** iBooks Author figures out the *y* axis's start value, end value, and increments automatically for you. But you can change those automatic values by entering your own in the Min and Max fields, and by setting the number of major increments in the Steps field (if the scale is linear) or Decades field (if the scale is logarithmic). For linear increments, you can also specify the number of minor increments that you want between major increments (appearing as minor tick marks and/or minor gridlines).

✔ **Value display settings:** These options control the display of the numeric values on the *y* axis. Check the Separator option to have a comma (in North American notation) or space (in European notation) appear in values of thousands or greater. Use the Format pop-up menu's options to set the numeric presentation, such as currency or percentages; you can create custom value formats by using the Custom option, explained in the section "Creating Custom Values," later in this chapter. Use the Decimals field or stepper controls to set the number of decimal places that you want to appear in the data values. Use the adjacent unnamed pop-up menu (think of it as the Negative Values pop-up menu) to choose whether negative numbers appear with a minus sign (–) or in parentheses; the default is to use minus signs. Use the Suffix field to add text after the numbers in the *y* axis; for example, if the values represent cubic centimeters, you might enter **cc** in the Suffix field.

✔ **Category Axis (X):** This pop-up menu has the same options as the Value Axis (Y) pop-up menu.

✔ **Label Every __ Categories:** Use this field or its stepper controls to determine which groups of bars get their data series labels along the *x* axis; the default Auto setting figures out how many of such labels fit the available space and then places the data in whatever increments allows such a fit. You can override this calculation by entering a specific value: 1 shows the labels for every group, 2 for every other group, and so on.

If you're working with a chart type where the bars extend from the left side rather than from the bottom, the Category Axis (Y) pop-up menu is renamed Category Axis (X) and the Category Axis (X) pop-up menu is renamed Category Axis (Y).

The options in the Series pane, shown in Figure 5-5, control the display of the labels for the chart's series data:

- ✔ **Value Labels:** Check this option to display the values for each bar. Use the four Position icon buttons to determine where these values appear: at the top of the bar, in the middle of the bar, at the bottom of the bar, or above the bar. You can control how the numbers themselves appear by using the Format, Decimals, Negative Display, and Separator fields described in the preceding list.

- ✔ **Trendline:** If you're working with any 2D bar chart (except stacked bar charts) and you click the Advanced disclosure triangle, an additional section appears. Its Trendline subpane lets you specify whether and how a trend line for your data appears over the bar chart. The unnamed pop-up menu lets you specify the trend line's scale: Linear, Logarithmic, Polynomial, Power, Exponential, and Moving Average.

  For a moving average, the adjacent Period field and its stepper controls let you remove the moving average's fluctuation for the specified period. Likewise, for a polynomial, the adjacent Order field and its stepper control lets you set the trend line's ascending or descending order.

  Check the Label option to display a label for the trend line in the legend and enter the label text in the adjacent field. To show the reader the mathematical calculation behind the trend line, check the Show Equation field (note it is not available for moving averages). To show the reader the R^2 value, check the Show R^2 Value option.

  The R^2 *value* is the coefficient of determination used in regression testing to determine how well the data fits the curve. In plain English, the closer the R^2 value is to 1, the better the data fits the curve and thus the more accurately the curve shows the actual trend.

- ✔ **Error Bars:** Also visible only if the Advanced section is displayed (as in Figure 5-6), the Error Bars subpane lets you display error bars over the bars. Error bars show the degree of possible deviation or margin of error for each bar's data. In the top unnamed pop-up menu in this subpane, choose the type of error-bar display you want: None, Positive and Negative, Positive Only, or Negative Only. In the following unnamed pop-up menu, choose the type of deviation you want displayed: Fixed Value, Percentage, Standard Deviation, or Standard Error. In the adjacent field, specify the value for the chosen deviation type, or use the stepper controls to change how the fixed, percentage, or standard deviation value is calculated. The Custom option lets you create your own numeric formatting, as explained in the section "Creating Custom Values," later in this chapter. Any custom formats previously defined also appear in this pop-up menu's options.

The Custom option doesn't always let you create your own formatting in iBooks Author. If the option is grayed out and thus not available, create a custom value in a table instead. Creating a custom value in a table forces the Custom option to Function in the Error Bar subpane's bottom pop-up menu.

Figure 5-6: The Chart inspector's Series pane for a line chart.

Line charts

The Chart inspector's Chart pane for line charts has just two options: Show Title and Show Legend, which work the same as they do for bar charts. Likewise, the Axis pane options for line charts are the same as for bar charts. (See the preceding section.) But the Series pane (shown in Figure 5-6) differs in several respects:

- ✔ **Data Symbol:** This pop-up menu lets you choose the type of indicator for the points on the line; it offers five shapes for line charts, as well as the option to have no point indicator. The adjacent field and stepper controls let you control the size of the point indicators.

- ✔ **Connect Points:** This pop-up menu lets you choose whether the lines between data points are straight or curved.

- ✔ **Value Labels:** The controls are the same as described in the preceding section for bar charts, except that there two sets of icon buttons to position the labels on line charts: Left, Center, and Right for horizontal positioning and Above, Middle, and

Below for vertical positioning. You set the vertical and horizontal positions separately, which gives you nine possible
locations for the labels.

✔ **Trendline:** The Trendline subpane's options are the same as
for 2D bar charts (and are likewise available only for 2D line
charts). (The Error Bar subpane's options are the same as for
bar charts.)

Area charts

The options for area charts are the same as for line charts (see the
preceding section), with these exceptions:

✔ Standard area charts don't have a Connect Points pop-up menu.

✔ Stacked area charts don't have the Connect Points pop-up
menu.

✔ The options in the Trendline subpane are grayed out (meaning they're unavailable).

Mixed bar-and-line charts

iBooks Author lets you create bar-and-line charts that let you
specify for each data series whether it appears as a line, bars, or
an area: Click a data series' element in your chart, and then choose
the desired display type from the Series pop-up menu: Column,
Line, or Area. Figure 5-7 shows the Chart inspector's Series pane
for a mixed bar-and-line chart.

The Chart and Axis panes for mixed charts are the same as for bar
charts (see the section "Bar charts," earlier in this chapter). But
the Series pane works differently to handle the mixture of presentation types:

✔ **Bar display:** The options for a bar series are the same as for
bar charts, described in the section "Bar charts," earlier in
this chapter.

✔ **Line display:** The options for a line series are the same as for
line charts, described in the section "Line charts," earlier in
this chapter.

✔ **Area display:** The options for an area are the same as for
regular area charts, described in the preceding section.

If you create a two-axis mixed chart, one additional control
appears in the Series pane: the Plot On pop-up menu, which lets
you specify which of the two y axes the chart's bars, lines, and
areas are plotted against (as well as which y axis appears).

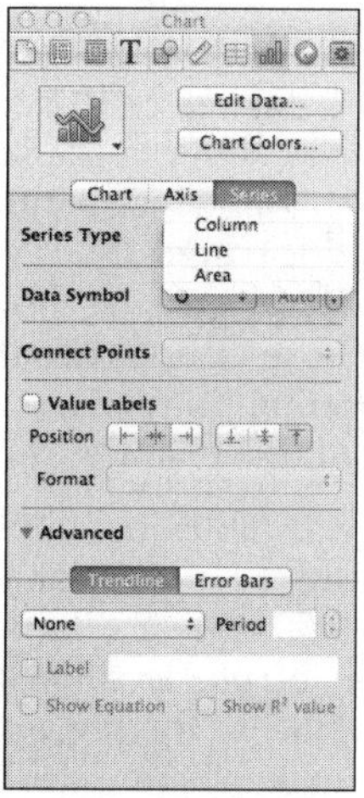

Figure 5-7: The Chart inspector's Series pane for a mixed bar-and-line chart.

Scatterplot charts

The Chart inspector's Chart pane for scatterplots has just two options: Show Title and Show Legend, which work the same as they do for bar charts (see the section "Bar charts," earlier in this chapter).

The Axis pane lacks the Label Every __ Categories option available for bar and line charts, but for a scatterplot chart, you can set the scale value and value display settings for the x axis, not just the y axis, unlike for bar and line charts.

The Series pane differs from bar charts in several ways:

- ✔ **Data Symbol:** This pop-up menu lets you choose the type of indicator for the points on the line; you can choose from seven shapes, as well as the option to have no point indicator. The adjacent field and stepper controls let you control the size of the point indicators.

- ✔ **Connect Points:** This pop-up menu lets you choose whether the lines between data points are straight or curved.

- ✔ **Trendline:** The Trendline subpane lets you specify separate trend lines for the x and y axes; bar charts and line charts display only trend lines for the data on the y axis. (The Error Bar subpane's options are the same as for bar and line charts, as described in the section "Bar charts," earlier in this chapter.)

Pie charts

If you're working with a pie chart, the Chart inspector has no panes, just the common options (which I cover in the section "All charts," earlier in this chapter) and the following sections, shown in Figure 5-8:

✔ **Show Title and Show Legend:** These options are the same as for the Chart pane for other presentation types, covered in the section "Bar charts," earlier in this chapter.

✔ **Labels:** Select this option to display labels containing the numeric data on each wedge in the pie chart. Use the Position slider to determine where the labels appear relative to the pie's center; the minimum 30% value places them near the center, 100% places them at the edge of the pie, and the maximum 200% value places them far outside the pie. If you want the axis labels for the data series to appear with those numeric values, select the Show Series Name option. The other settings — Format, Decimals, Negative Display, and Separator — work the same as in a bar chart's Axis pane, described in the section "Bar charts," earlier in this chapter.

✔ **Wedges:** This section appears in the Chart inspector. Use the Explode slider, field, or stepper controls if you want to *explode* the pie chart's wedges — that is, push them out from the center. Note that a value of 0% keeps the wedges together. You can rotate the pie by using the Rotation Angle wheel, field, or stepper controls. A value of 0° (the default) has the first data series element's wedge begin at the top-center of the pie, and the rest follow. Specify an (optional) drop shadow for the whole group or just the selected wedge by using the Shadow pop-up menu.

3D charts

If you're working with 3D charts, an additional section called 3D Scene appears in the Chart inspector for pie charts (as shown in Figure 5-8) and in the Chart inspector's Chart pane for bar, line, and bar-and-line charts. (There are no 3D presentation options for scatterplots.) Its options are

✔ **3D Position:** Drag the pointer through the 3D Position bubble (marked with crossed two-way arrows) to rotate the chart to any rotation angle desired.

✔ **Lighting Style:** Use this pop-up menu to determine how the simulated lighting appears on the chart's objects. The options are Default, Glossy, Medium Center, Medium Left, Medium Right, Soft Fill, and Soft Light.

✔ **Chart Depth:** Use this slider to give the chart elements simulated depth; the more you move the slider to the right, the more dimension appears for the objects. To have the objects appear paper thin, move the slider all the way to the left.

✔ **Show Bevel Edges:** Select this option to give objects in 3D bar and pie charts a beveled (diagonally cut) edge. (This option isn't available for 3D line charts.)

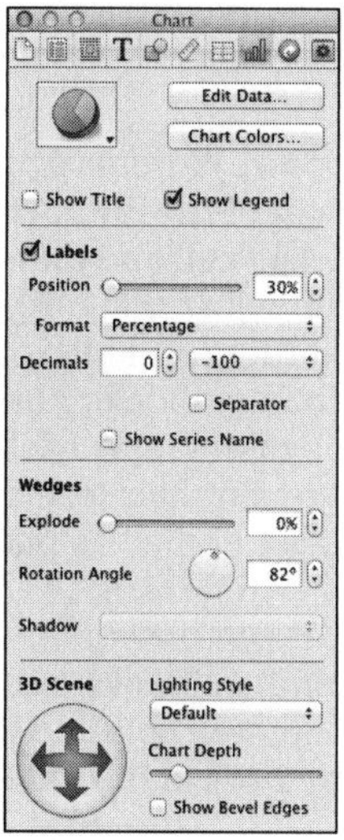

Figure 5-8: The options in the Chart inspector for pie charts, as well as for 3D charts of any presentation type.

Creating, Editing, and Formatting Tables

The table is a time-honored way to show data where, like charts, two axes appear, against which information can be categorized. Although charts deal with numeric information, tables usually deal with textual information (although they can also deal with numeric information, such as in the case of spreadsheets).

The tables you create in iBooks Author are very much like those you might create in a word processor or desktop publishing program, and most of the controls will be familiar, even if they reside in different arrangements than you're used to. But iBooks Author does provide two types of controls uncommon in other programs.

One is the ability to add formulas that do calculations based on the table's data. The other is to format a cell conditionally based on its text's characteristics.

The following sections explain the common formatting and editing controls. Many of the formatting options for cells apply to rows, columns, and even the entire table, depending on what you select before you apply them.

Formatting tables

When you add a document from Microsoft Word or Apple Pages as a new chapter in iBooks Author, most of the formatting in the document's tables is preserved, including cell and table borders, shading, and text formatting — but not cell spacing. If you copy a spreadsheet selection into iBooks Author from Microsoft Excel, none of the formatting is retained, although iBooks Author does apply every-other-row shading to such tables. Spreadsheet selections copied from Apple Numbers do retain their formatting. And tables copied from other applications are copied as plain text, without their tabular arrangement.

To format a table (or refine its formatting) in iBooks Author, you use the Table inspector, which has two panes — Table and Format — as shown in Figure 5-9. You do most of the work in the Table pane.

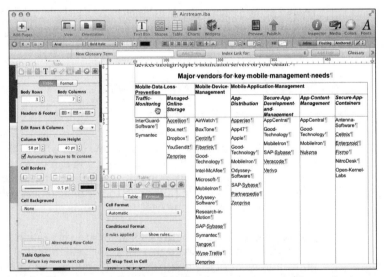

Figure 5-9: The Table inspector Table and Format panes, as well as a simple table.

Most of the table-specific formatting controls reside in the Table inspector's Table pane:

- ✔ **Body Rows and Body Columns:** Use these fields and their stepper controls to specify the number of rows and columns for your table. Imported and pasted tables have these values already specified based on their contents. You can also add rows and columns by using the Edit Rows & Columns pop-up menu described in the section "Sorting, adding, and deleting," later in this chapter.

- ✔ **Headers & Footers:** Use the three icon menus in this section — Column, Header, and Footer — to add the specified number of header columns, header rows, and footer rows to the table. (These options are also available by choosing Format⇨Table and choosing from the submenu that appears.) You can add as many as five; to remove a header or footer, choose 0 (zero).

  If your table already has headers and/or footers, using these icon menus doesn't place their contents in the new headers or footers; you need to cut and paste their text into the header and footers manually.

  An additional control in the Header icon menu appears if your table is an inline object: the Repeat Header Rows on Each Page option. If selected (a check mark appears to its left), the header row is supposed to repeat on any page the table continues onto; however, iBooks Author 1.1 and earlier have no mechanism for creating a table that goes across multiple pages (such as one too long to fit on one page), so this option, in effect, does nothing.

- ✔ **Borders:** If you select the entire table (click its upper-left corner to make the selection handles appear for the whole table), you can click any of the Cell Borders icon buttons to apply those borders to the entire table.

- ✔ **Return Key Moves to Next Cell:** If this option is selected and you're working on a cell's text, pressing Return moves the pointer to the next cell down — and adds a row when you reach the bottom of the table. Otherwise, pressing Return adds a paragraph return within the cell.

You can specify a few table-wide settings elsewhere:

- ✔ Set a single stroke size for all table borders in a selected table by using the Stroke options in the Graphic inspector, as explained in Chapter 4.

- ✔ Apply a caption and title to the table, as described in the section "Adding Object Captions and Titles," earlier in this chapter; you can also set attributes such as a background and drop shadow.

✔ Apply a background fill to a table by selecting all its cells and using the Cell Background pop-up menu's options; if you select the table (so that you see its selection handles), the Cell Background pop-up menu is unavailable.

After you format a table, you can copy its formatting to other tables by following these steps:

1. **Select the table whose style you want to copy.**

2. **Choose Format⇨Copy Table Style.**

   Alternatively, you can press Option+⌘+C.

3. **Select the table to which you want to apply the first table's style.**

4. **Choose Format⇨Paste Style.**

   Or you can press Option+⌘+V.

You can also set a table's formatting as the default for all future tables by selecting that table and then choosing Format⇨Advanced⇨Define Default Table Style, and you can apply that saved format to an existing table by selecting the table and then choosing Format⇨Reapply Defaults to Table.

You can resize a table by selecting it and dragging its selection handles. If the table is an inline object (see Chapter 2), you can adjust only the table's width. Be sure that the entire table is selected, rather than a row or column border; otherwise, only that row or column is resized.

You can convert tabbed text so that it becomes a table by selecting the text and then choosing Format⇨Table⇨Convert Text to Table. Each tab begins a new column, and each paragraph break begins a new row. Likewise, you can convert a table into tabbed text by choosing Format⇨Table⇨Convert Table to Text.

Formatting and editing columns and rows

In the Table inspector's Table pane, you can format and edit columns and rows. The Table pane has two basic types of controls available:

✔ The cell-formatting controls for borders and fills (which you can also apply to entire rows and columns, if you select the entire row or column)

✔ The controls to add, delete, and sort rows and columns

To select a cell, simply click in it; to select multiple cells, Shift-drag across the cells you want to select. To select an entire row or column, choose Format⇨Table⇨Select Row or Format⇨Table⇨Select Column. You also can choose Select Row or Select Column in the Table pane's Edit Rows & Columns pop-up menu.

Formatting borders and backgrounds

I cover the cell-formatting controls in the section "Formatting and editing cells," later in this chapter, with these two exceptions, which apply to rows and columns, not just cells:

✔ **Alternating Row Color:** Select this option to have iBooks Author apply a fill to every other row in the table. Click the swatch to the left of this option to open the Colors panel, where you can choose a color, as explained in Chapter 4.

✔ **Row and column lines:** Select a row or column border in the table, and then use the Cell Borders controls described in the section "Formatting and editing cells," later in this chapter, to apply a stroke weight and color to the selected line.

Resizing

You can resize columns and rows in several ways:

✔ Select a row or column's border, and then drag it to resize that row or column.

✔ Select any cell in a column or row, and then use the Column Width or Row Height fields or stepper controls in the Text pane to change the size.

✔ Select the Automatically Resize to Fit Content option in the Text pane to have rows' depth increase to fit their text; the cell with the most text determines the row's overall depth.

Sorting, adding, and deleting

You can use the Edit Rows & Columns pop-up menu to do additional row and column manipulations: sorting, adding, and deleting. You also can access all except the sort options by choosing Format⇨Table and choosing an option from the submenu that appears:

✔ **Sort Ascending and Sort Descending:** If you select cells within a column, choosing one of these menu options sorts those cells' rows alphabetically based on the values in those selected cells. Sort Ascending sorts in the order A to Z or 0 to 9, whereas Sort Descending sorts in the order Z to A or 9 to 0. If you select cells across more than one column, these options are unavailable.

✔ **Add Row Above, Add Row Below, Add Column Before, and Add Column After:** Add the row or column as specified from the currently selected cell. The keyboard shortcuts are Option+up arrow for Add Row Above, Option+down arrow for Add Row Below, Option+left arrow for Add Column Before, and Option+right arrow for Add Column After.

✔ **Delete Row and Delete Column:** Remove the specified item based on the currently selected cells' location.

Distributing

You can access one row and column formatting option only by choosing Format⟹Table and choosing an option from the submenu that appears. The Distribute Rows Evenly and Distribute Columns Evenly menu options even out the spacing for the selected cells' rows or columns, respectively.

If you want to even out the spacing of the entire table's rows or columns, select the entire table, rather than specific cells.

Formatting and editing cells

Editing cells is simple: Double-click the cell to add or edit its contents. Press Tab to move from left to right from cell to cell (or to the first item in the following row) and Shift+Tab to move from right to left from cell to cell (or to the last item in the preceding row). You apply formatting and styles to cell text just like you do any text, as explained in Chapter 3.

The rest of the table tools relate to formatting cells or their contents. Most are split between the Table inspector's Table pane and its Format pane; you have to access a few of the tools elsewhere.

Merging and splitting cells

The Table pane's Edit Rows & Columns pop-up menu (as well as the submenu that appears when you choose Format⟹Table) has two options related to selected cells:

✔ **Merge Cells:** Merge the currently selected cells. The contents of all the cells are retained in the merged cell; a tab is inserted for each blank cell in the selection.

✔ **Split Columns and Split Rows:** Divide the currently selected cell into two columns or two rows, depending on your choice.

Formatting borders and backgrounds

The Table inspector's Table pane has two related controls that apply to the selected cells in the table:

✓ **Cell Borders:** Use the eight icon buttons to apply a *stroke* (line) to the designated area of your selected cells. Select the stroke type (None, Thin, Medium, Dashed, or Dotted) in the unnamed pop-up menu below the buttons, enter the stroke weight in the unnamed field or use its stepper controls, and specify the color by clicking the adjacent swatch to open the Colors panel described Chapter 4.

✓ **Cell Background:** In this pop-up menu, the Color Fill option puts a solid color as the cell's background, and Color Gradient puts a gradient fill as the background. The controls that you use to select the color or define the gradient are described in Chapter 4. (The iBooks Author help system says it offers an option to place an image file as the background; that capability isn't enabled in iBooks Author 1.1 or earlier.)

In the Table inspector's Format pane, select the Wrap Text in Cell option to allow text to break across multiple lines to fit in the cell. If this option is deselected and Automatically Resize to Fit Contents is deselected in the Table pane, text that doesn't fit in the cell gets cut off, so only part of it appears.

Formatting values

You can set the formatting for the numerals and other values in your table in the Format pane's Cell Format pop-up menu. The default values are similar to those used in charts, with a few additions: Automatic (iBooks Author figures out the appropriate format based on the cell's values), Number, Currency, Percentage, Data and Time, Duration, Fraction, Numeral System (which lets you set the base, such as base 8 for octal values and 16 for hexadecimal values), Scientific, and Text. (The Numeral System and Text options aren't available for charts.)

Any custom value formats defined in previous tables or charts in the current e-book also appear, as does the Custom option (explained in the section "Creating Custom Values," later in this chapter) to create additional value formats.

Each value format has its own options to control its specific display. For example, if you choose Currency, you can select which currency symbol to use, whether to include separators in values larger than 999, how to handle negative values, how many decimal places to display, and whether to use accounting style (which places a tab between the currency symbol and the value, aligning the value on its decimal).

Using conditional formats

Unlike most other layout programs, iBooks Author allows you to set rules for conditional formatting of a cell's contents. (Numbers does have this capability, and Excel has a similar capability.)

You add conditional formatting rules to a cell by following these steps:

1. **Click the Show Rules button in the Table inspector's Format pane.**

   The Conditional Format panel appears.

2. **Choose an option from the Choose a Rule pop-up menu.**

   There are three groups of rules in the pop-up menu's options. Based on the type of rule you choose, an additional option in which you specify the scope of the rule appears.

   You can enter a formula in the fields for any of the groups of rules. After you choose a function, click the icon that appears to the right of the field (inside the field boundaries); it looks like a cell with a + (plus sign) on its lower-right corner. You can now enter a formula, text, and cell references like you would in a spreadsheet program. Click the red X icon that appears to clear the formula.

3a. **If you choose one of the Boolean logical functions, enter the appropriate values in the one or two fields that appear to the right of the pop-up menu (based on the option chosen).**

   The Boolean logical functions available are Equal To, Not Equal To, Greater Than, Less Than, Greater Than or Equal To, Less Than or Equal To, Between, and Not Between. If you choose Between or Not Between, two fields appear; otherwise, one field appears. For example, if you choose Greater Than, you enter the value in the field that needs to be true for the formatting to be applied, such as **10** if you want the formatting applied to all cells whose value is greater than 10.

3b. **If you choose one of the text-evaluation functions, enter the text to be evaluated in the field that appears to the right of the pop-up menu.**

   The text-evaluation functions are Text Contains, Text Doesn't Contain, Text Starts With, Text Ends With, and Text Is. For example, if you choose Text Doesn't Contain and enter **None** in the adjacent field, the formatting is applied to all cells whose text doesn't contain the letter sequence None (including Nonetheless, Nonentity, and so on).

3c. If you choose the sole date-evaluation function, choose a date in the With Dates pop-up menu.

The date options are words, such as Today, In the Next, and Between. Some of these options cause other options to appear. For example, if you choose In the Next, a third pop-up menu appears with the options Week, Month, and Year. And if you choose Between, two text fields appear, one for each of the dates you want to date range to be between; enter dates in **mm/dd/yyyy** format.

4. If you want to add another rule, click the + (plus sign) icon button.

Another Choose a Rule pop-up menu appears. Follow the appropriate Step 3 to specify that rule's conditions. You can continue to add rules by clicking the + (plus sign) icon button after the rule where you want to add the new rule.

5. Click the Edit button to specify the formatting that's applied if that condition is met.

Clicking this button displays swatches for the text color and cell fill, and icon buttons that you can use to apply boldface, italics, and strikethrough to the cell's text, as shown at the bottom of Figure 5-10.

6. Click Done to apply the formatting.

You can select a rule and click Edit to change its formatting.

7. Click the Conditional Format panel's Close box when done to set the conditions.

In the Table inspector's Format pane, the text *X* Rules Applied appears to the left of the Show Rules button so that you know rules have been applied (*X* is replaced by the number of rules applied).

You can edit an existing set of rules and the formatting that gets applied if the conditions are met by selecting the cells that have the rules applied and then clicking the Show Rule button in the Format pane to open the Conditional Format panel. In that panel, select the rule you want to modify and change its settings, and/or click its Edit button to change its formatting.

To remove a rule in the Conditional Format panel, select a rule and click the – (minus sign) icon button to delete it. (Click Clear All Rules to delete all the rules at the same time.)

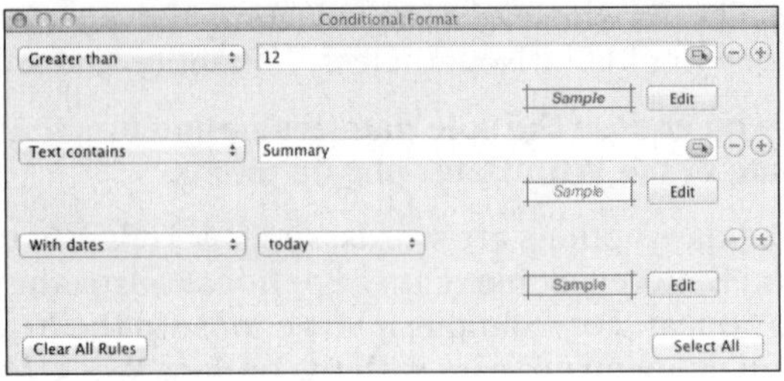

Figure 5-10: A cell condition that has three rules.

Copying formatting and values

You can copy and paste cells' contents into other cells to copy their data, cell formats, formulas, and color fills — just like you would in Excel or Numbers:

- ✔ Choose Edit➪Copy (or press ⌘+C), click the pointer in another cell, then choose Edit➪Paste (or press ⌘+V) to paste the cell's contents and formatting into that other cell.

- ✔ Choose Edit➪Copy (or press ⌘+C), click the pointer outside the table, and then choose Edit➪Paste (or press ⌘+V) to paste the cell's contents and formatting into a new table object at the pointer's location.

- ✔ Drag the table's cells outside the table to have iBooks Author create a new table composed from copies of those cells.

But iBooks Author has two other options to let you copy formatting and text values from one cell to another using what it calls a fill operation. Here's how they work (it's different than in Excel but the same as in Numbers):

- ✔ Select a cell and drag the fill handle (a tiny circle in the cell's lower-right corner) to the right and/or down over the cells into which you want to paste the data, cell formats, formulas, and color fills used in the selected cell. Any data in the cells you drag the fill handle over have their data replaced with the value you're pasting.

  Likewise, to continue a pattern to other cells (for example, if a cell contains a day of the week), select the cell and drag its fill handle to the right and/or down. And to continue a numeric pattern, select two or more cells before dragging. For example, if you select cells containing 1 and 2, the values 3 and 4 are added when you drag through the adjacent two cells. If you select cells containing 1 and 4, the values 7 and 10 are added to the adjacent cells (the values are incremented by 3 because the initial values were 1 and 4).

✔ Select one or more cells in the same row or column, and then select two or more adjacent cells. Then, choose Format⇨Table⇨Fill and choose one of the following options from the submenu that appears:

- *Fill Right:* Assigns selected cells the value that resides in the leftmost selected cell.

- *Fill Left:* Assigns selected cells the value that resides in the rightmost selected cell.

- *Fill Up:* Assigns selected cells the value that resides in the bottommost selected cell.

- *Fill Down:* Assigns selected cells the value that resides in the topmost selected cell.

Using functions

You can let iBooks Author do the math for you within tables, just like you can in Excel or Numbers. But the e-book's readers can't adjust the calculations to experiment with values; instead, the calculations are a convenience for you, the author, to save some calculation effort.

There are three basic ways to apply formulas to cells in iBooks Author, and the first two begin in the Table inspector's Format pane:

✔ Select the cells to which you want to apply the formula, and then choose the desired calculation from the Formula pop-up menu: None, Sum, Min (minimum value in the set), Max (maximum value in the set), Average, Count (number of values in the set), and Product (which multiplies all the values in the set against each other).

If the cell selection goes across two or more rows, a new row is inserted below the selected cells, and each cell contains the results for the selected cells above. If the cell selection goes across two or more columns but just one row, a new column is inserted to the right of the selected cells, showing the formula's results in the adjacent cell.

✔ Select a cell in which you want to place the results of a calculation, and then choose the desired calculation from the Formula pop-up menu or choose the Formula Editor option to enter your own calculation. Figure 5-11 shows the Formula Editor.

The Formula Editor lets you create more complex calculations, such as adding values across several rows and columns (to choose cells as inputs to your formula, you can drag-select the cells, as well as select individual cells with the pointer) — just like in Excel or Numbers. You can also use a variety of other formulas, including trigonometric, accounting, and logical (if) formulas — also like Excel and Numbers, including the same syntax that you would use in Excel or Numbers. Some portions of the formula have options you can apply; look for a small down-pointing triangle to the right of the colored portions and click it to reveal its menu options, as shown in Figure 5-11.

After you enter the formula in the Formula Editor, click the green checkmark icon (which appears to the right of the formula) to enter it or the red X icon (next to the green checkmark) to clear it, as shown in Figure 5-11. Double-click an existing formula to edit it in the Formula Editor.

✔ Select a cell and choose Insert➪Function, and then choose the desired formula, Formula Editor, or — available only here — Show Function Browser. The formulas and Formula Editor work just like they do in the preceding method. If you choose Show Function Browser, the Formula Editor appears over your selected cell, and the Function Browser, shown in Figure 5-11, appears onscreen to give you a list of all the formulas available in iBooks Author, so you don't have to rely on memory. Select a category from the list at left to see the available functions; click one to get a description of its use. Click the Insert Function button to add that selected function to the Formula Editor.

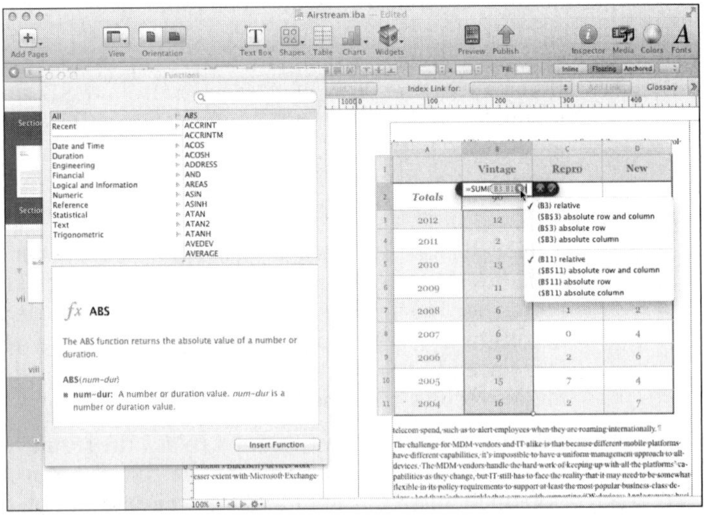

Figure 5-11: Enter a formula via the Formula Editor (the Function Browser at left shows the available formulas).

Working with Custom Values

When formatting chart and table values, some pop-up menus provide the Custom option for creating your own value presentation styles, known as custom values:

✔ For several kinds of charts, you use the Format pop-up menu in the Chart inspector's Axis pane for the *y* axis's value presentation (see the section "Bar charts," earlier in this chapter).

✔ For several kinds of charts, you use the second (unnamed) pop-up menu in the Error Bars subpane of the Chart inspector's Axis pane for the error bar's value presentation (also see the section "Bar charts," earlier in this chapter).

✔ For tables, you use the Cell Format pop-up menu in the Table inspector's Format pane for the cell's value presentation (see the section "Formatting values," earlier in this chapter).

A custom value would be *yyyy/mm/dd*, such as 2012/03/16 to indicate March 16, 2012, or *xx*°K, such as 32°K to indicate 32 degrees Kelvin.

Creating custom values

In all three cases, if you choose the Custom menu option, you get a settings sheet shown in Figure 5-12. The settings sheet has two variants, as the figure shows:

✔ Number & Text

✔ Date & Time

Use the Type pop-up menu to switch between the two variants.

Universal custom value options

Both variants of the settings sheet for custom values contain the Name field, where you give the value format a unique name, which appears in the Cell Format pop-up menu for tables, the Format pop-up menu for value labels in charts, and the unnamed pop-up menu for setting error bars in charts.

Also common to the two variants are the Cancel and OK buttons (OK saves the new format).

Both variants also have the Manage Formats button. Don't use this button when you set up custom values; as explained in the "Editing custom values" section, later in this chapter, you use it only after you define your custom formats, *never* while you're doing so.

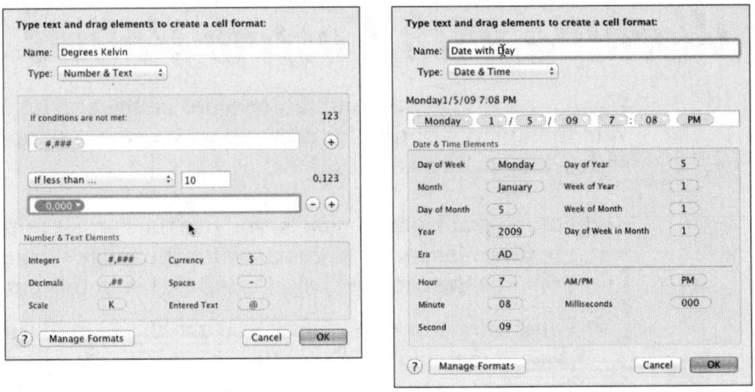

Figure 5-12: The settings sheet for creating value formats for numbers and text (left) and for dates and times (right).

Whatever kind of value format you're creating or editing, after you make your changes, click OK to save it or Cancel to not save it.

Number & Text settings

For numbers and text, you can set up various conditions. The first condition applies to any numbers that don't match the other conditions; it is the default condition. Drag any of the number and text elements (those with blue oval backgrounds) into the condition field to have that element appear in the cell. You can also enter your own text. For example, typing **No.** and then dragging in the integers element (#,###) displays No. 12 if the cell's value is 12.

Click the + (plus sign) icon to add additional conditions, choosing the desired one from the pop-up menu that appears. In the field below, construct the formatting results for that condition by using the number and text elements at the bottom of the settings sheet. Some elements display a down-pointing triangle to the right when you drag them into the field, indicating the element has a pop-up menu of further options from which you can choose.

You can add additional conditions and their formatting by clicking the + (plus sign) icon button for each desired condition. Select a condition and click the – (minus sign) icon button to delete it. Figure 5-12 shows an example of a numeric condition.

Date & Time settings

For dates and times, the settings sheet has no conditions, just the format in which you want the date and/or time to appear, as Figure 5-12 shows. Drag into the field the date and time elements from which you want to compose the presentation, in the order you want them to appear. (You can rearrange the elements in the field by dragging them.) Some elements display a down-pointing triangle to the right when you drag it into the field, indicating it has a pop-up menu of further options from which you can choose.

Applying custom values

After you create a custom value, it's available as a menu option in the following pop-up menus:

- ✔ The Format pop-up menu in the Chart inspector's Axis (see the section "Bar charts," earlier in this chapter).

- ✔ The second (unnamed) pop-up menu in the Error Bars sub-pane of the Chart inspector's Axis pane (also see the section "Bar charts," earlier in this chapter).

- ✔ For tables, the Cell Format pop-up menu in the Table inspector's Format pane (see the section "Formatting values," earlier in this chapter).

Editing custom values

The process of editing a value format's settings is the same as creating that format (as described in the section "Setting up custom values," earlier in this chapter).

But you can do one other type of editing to value formats: Modify the menu options that appear in the pop-up menus that let you apply value formats. You use the Manage Formats button in the settings sheet to edit the list of formats that appears in pop-up menus — to delete value formats that you no longer want to be available and to change the order of how the value formats appear. Follow these steps:

1. **In the appropriate pop-up menu (see the preceding section), choose Format.**

   The settings sheet described in the "Setting up custom values" section, earlier in this chapter, opens, displaying the current settings.

2. **Click the Manage Formats button.**

   A new settings sheet appears.

3a. **To delete a custom value, select it and click its adjacent – (minus sign) icon button.**

3b. To change where a value format appears in pop-up menus that use it, select that value format, and then click the appropriate arrow icon button.

Clicking the down-arrow icon button moves the value format option down the list one increment, and clicking the up-arrow icon button to move it up the list one increment.

Keep clicking the appropriate icon button until the value format is in the desired position. Move other value format options in the list the same way.

3c. To rename a value format, double-click it and enter the new name.

You also can change the name of a value format by changing its name in the Name field, described in the "Universal custom value settings" section, earlier in this chapter, rather than by clicking the Manage Formats button.

4. Click the OK button to save the changes and close the settings sheet.

Or click Cancel to leave the value format unchanged.

Using Shapes and Lines

You can use shapes — such as lines, circles, squares, and speech bubbles — for traditional (static) infographics. iBooks Author provides 15 predefined shapes, plus the Pen tool that you can use to draw your own lines and shapes, using a method called Bézier. (A Bézier pen tool is the standard pen tool in almost every illustration application and is widely used in many other programs' drawing functions.)

You might use shapes for one of two reasons:

- As a graphical embellishment in a layout, such as having a blue square next to all chapter titles
- As part of a diagram or other illustration composed of multiple shapes and text boxes

Using predefined shapes

Adding a shape is simple: Choose one from the Shapes icon menu in the toolbar, or choose Insert⇨Shape and choose one from the submenu that appears. Figure 5-13 shows all the shapes available.

Here's what you can do with shapes (all of these techniques are explained in Chapter 4):

- ✔ Resize it and move it like any object.

- ✔ Add a fill (including an image, to create a cameo effect), change the border's stroke, give it a drop shadow, and change its transparency level like you can with other objects by using the Graphic inspector or in the Format bar. (If the Format bar isn't visible below the toolbar, choose View➪Show Format Bar or press Shift+⌘+R.)

- ✔ Add text wrap around a shape, just like you can with any other object, by using the Wrap inspector.

- ✔ Flip the shape by using the Flip Horizontally and Flip Vertically menu options in the Arrange menu and in the Metrics inspector.

- ✔ Rotate a shape via the controls in the Metrics inspector or by ⌘-dragging a selection handle.

But there's a major difference between manipulating shapes and most other objects: When you drag a selection handle, you reshape the shape, you don't resize it proportionally. To resize a shape proportionally, hold Shift while dragging any selection handle. (Text boxes, explained in Chapter 3, work the same way as shapes in this regard, by the way.)

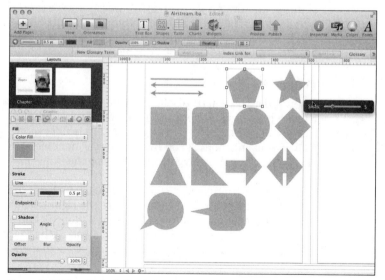

Figure 5-13: The 15 predefined shapes available in iBooks Author.

Finally, you can enter text into a shape; just double-click it. Thus, you don't have to overlap text boxes onto shapes to make labeled shapes.

And here's a secret: iBooks Author really has just 8 shapes available; 7 of the 15 shapes presented in the menus are in fact variations of existing shapes that you can create yourself, as I explain in the following sections.

Straight lines

The line, line with single arrowhead, and line with two arrowheads are actually all the same shape: a straight line. You specify whether a line has arrowheads (and what type of arrowhead; there are 10 types) by choosing the desired style from the two Endpoint pop-up menus in the format bar or from the two Endpoint pop-up menus in the Graphic inspector's Stroke section. The one-arrowhead line and the double-arrowhead line shapes in the Shape icon menu and Insert⇨Shape submenu are just lines with the endpoints pre-applied for you.

Unlike other shapes, you can rotate lines, not just stretch them or shorten them. Drag an endpoint up or down to rotate the line in that direction.

Squares and circles

If you add a rounded square and select it, a blue circle appears near its upper-left corner. Drag that circle all the way to the left to convert the edges into 90-degree corners (making a regular square), and drag it all the way to the right to convert the square into a circle. The square and circle shapes in the Shape icon menu and Insert⇨Shape submenu are fixed, so you can't adjust their corners' curvature. (Chapter 4 explains corner curvature.)

Polygons

If you add a polygon (the default is a pentagon, or five-sided polygon), a floating Sides slider appears. You can drag the slider to change the number of sides, from 3 (a triangle) to 11 (a hendecagon); sliding it to 4 gives you a diamond. (You can change the number of sides later by simply selecting the polygon and adjusting the slider.)

The separate triangle and square shapes can't have their number of sides changed. And you can't create the right-triangle shape by using the polygon shape (well, you can if you edit the shape, as explained in the section "Editing shapes and paths," later in this chapter — but that's going beyond changing a shape's attribute).

Stars

The star shape works like the polygon shape: The floating Points slider lets you change the number of points on the star from 3 (a triangle) to 20.

Right triangles

If you remember your high school geometry class, you remember a right triangle, where one vertex (corner) has a 90-degree angle, forming a squared-off corner. For some reason, few programs that offer preconfigured shapes offer a right triangle; they usually just offer the typical triangle where the top vertex is centered over the bottom side. But iBooks Author offers a right-triangle shape, in addition to the usual triangle shape.

Arrows

Not to be confused with a line that has an arrowhead (or two arrowheads), the two arrow shapes can be modified. One shape is a left-pointing arrow, and the other is a double arrow.

When you select an arrow, a blue circle appears on the upper side where the shaft meets the arrowhead. Move that circle to the side to change the relative lengths of the shaft and arrowhead, and up or down to change their thickness.

Speech bubbles

The two speech bubbles are really the same shape; one is set to have a circular shape and the other to a rounded-square shape. But you can reshape either one to the other, as well as to other variations.

When you select a speech bubble, three blue circle controls appear, which let you adjust the speech bubble. The one near the upper-left corner changes the bubble's curvature, from square to circle. The one where the cone intersects the bubble widens or narrows the cone. The one at the cone's point rotates and lengthens the cone.

Drawing with the Pen tool

Although Bézier-style pen tools are common in illustration applications, most people don't use such apps and so are unfamiliar with its drawing method. It's a bit odd to use the first few times when you want to draw curved lines because it doesn't work in the way you might expect. Follow these steps:

1. **Choose the Pen tool from the Shape icon menu.**

   Alternatively, you can choose it from the Insert➪Shape submenu.

2. **Click in your document where you want to set the starting point.**

3. **Click the second point, but don't release the pointer.**

4. **Drag the pointer.**

   The control handle appears.

5. **Rotate and adjust the length of the control handle to change the line segment's curve direction and pitch, as Figure 5-14 shows.**

6. **Release the pointer to create the curve.**

7. **Click and hold the next point, adjusting its curve the same way.**

8. **When you're done, double-click the starting point to create a closed shape.**

   Alternatively, press Esc to create an open shape, with the last point created becoming the endpoint.

You can edit a curve at any time by clicking one of its points and then dragging the control handle that appears.

If you don't do the click-and-hold routine, you get a straight line when you click the subsequent location, as you can see at the top of Figure 5-14. Of course, you can mix curved and straight segments in the same shape.

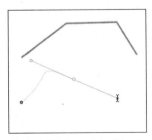

Figure 5-14: A straight-line shape (top) and a curved segment (bottom) created with the Bézier pen tool.

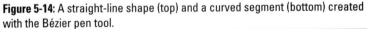

Editing shapes and paths

You can edit a shape beyond the controls described in the preceding sections to adjust various shapes. To do so, select the shape and choose Format⇨Shape⇨Make Editable. For a line, Bézier curve, or other shape, the selection handles disappear and red circles appear on the shape where that shape's *segments* (the lines between points) connect. For a Bézier curve or line, you can also simply click the curve after you select the shape, rather than use the menu command.

All you can do with a line is move its endpoints, and you can move those endpoints simply by selecting the line. Even if you use the Make Editable command or double-click the line, you can't do more than that, so why bother?

Figure 5-15 shows two examples, one a Bézier curve and one a predefined shape.

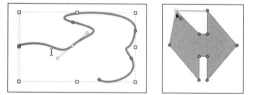

Figure 5-15: A Bézier curve being edited (left) and a predefined shape being edited (right).

Click any point to move it, which changes the shape that it's part of. The currently selected point is shown as a white circle, and all others are shown as red circles. Click another point to manipulate it. For Bézier curves and for curves on predefined shapes (such as circles and shapes with rounded corners), you can also manipulate the active point's control handle to change its segment's curve.

After you make a shape editable, it stays editable. To work on it later, just click to select it, and then click the edge or segment that you want to change to display its points for manipulation.

You can take two other related actions on an editable shape; these options are available for the selected shape in the submenu when you choose Format⇨Shape:

✔ **Smooth Path:** Converts straight segments in the shape to curves

✔ **Sharp Path:** Converts curved segments in the shape to straight lines

These commands affect all segments in a shape. If you want to convert just specific segments of a shape, you're out of luck.

If you make a curved shape sharp and then smooth it, you may not get the original shape; in fact, you're almost certain not to with a Bézier curve because this command makes the curves even, with no pitch to one side that most Bézier objects have.

Chapter 6

Working with Interactive Elements

- -

In This Chapter

▶ Adding images to iBooks Author

▶ Engaging the reader with video, audio, and slideshows

▶ Testing the reader's knowledge with quizzes

▶ Getting technical with web widgets

- -

*P*erhaps iBooks Author's most compelling attribute is its extensive support for objects with which e-book readers can interact. The concept predates iBooks Author, of course: For years, you've been able to embed videos, audio, and basic button-style interactions in PDF files, for example. But iBooks Author brings these capabilities and a raft of new ones — such as review quizzes, web widgets, and 3D images — to the world of e-books. Plus it makes some interactions — such as presentations, image galleries, and interactive graphics — much easier to create than in PDF-creation tools.

iBooks Author supports interactive objects, called widgets, which include image galleries, interactive graphics, 3D graphics, movies (meaning both video and audio files), Keynote presentations, reviews (quizzes), and web widgets (web-style components).

Chapter 4 explains how to format these objects' containers, and Chapter 5 explains how to arrange their captions, contents, and titles, so this chapter focuses on how to take advantage of the interactivity that each widget offers. This chapter also explains any requirements in creating the widgets' contents outside of iBooks Author. After all, the contents for several widget objects are created externally: movies, Keynote presentations, and 3D graphics. You create web widgets outside of iBooks Author, as well. And the source images for interactive images and image galleries also come from outside iBooks Author. So the only widget object you're guaranteed to create wholly within iBooks Author is a review.

Image Galleries

One of the simplest widget objects to create in an iBooks Author e-book is an image gallery, which lets readers move through a series of images at their pace in a slideshow-like presentation.

Adding gallery images

To add a gallery object, choose Gallery from the Widgets icon menu in the toolbar or choose Insert⇨Widget⇨Gallery. After you add the gallery object, you can add images in any of four ways:

- ✔ Drag one or more image files from a folder or disk in the Finder onto the gallery object.

- ✔ Drag one or more image files from the Finder onto the Gallery Media section of the Widget inspector's Interaction pane. (The Widget inspector automatically opens to the Interaction pane when you add a gallery object.)

- ✔ In the Widget inspector's Interaction pane, click the + (plus sign) icon button to open a settings sheet in which you can find and import an image; after selecting the desired image, click Insert. (You can add only one image at a time this way.)

- ✔ Choose Format⇨Gallery⇨Add Image to open the settings sheet from which you add an image.

You can add any supported image (see Chapter 4); if you add a PDF file, only the first page is displayed in the e-book's gallery. To build the image gallery, add all the desired images. The order in which you add them determines their order in the gallery, but you can change that order, as described in the following section.

However you add images to a gallery object, they also appear in the Gallery Media section of the Widget inspector's Interaction pane, which is shown in Figure 6-1 with an example gallery object.

Working with gallery images

iBooks Author lets you adjust several aspects of the images in your gallery object: their order in the gallery, their size and position within the gallery's image frame, and the shape of the image frame's corners. You can also remove images from a gallery.

Figure 6-1: An image gallery (right) is largely managed via the Widget inspector's Interaction pane (center).

To select a specific image in the gallery, such as to *mask* (crop) it, you can click its name in the Widget inspector's Interaction pane. Or you can click the right-arrow icon (to go forward) or the left-arrow icon (to go backward) in the gallery object itself; these icons appear below the current image in the gallery. When you reach the image you want to adjust, stop clicking the arrow icon.

Reordering images

You can change the order of images in the gallery by dragging an image's Reorder handle (the stack of three horizontal bars) up or down through the list in the Widget inspector's Interaction pane.

By default, an image gallery on the iPad displays whatever image currently appears in the iBooks Author document — the e-book doesn't default to the first image in the gallery, it defaults to the last one you had active in iBooks Author. So, before publishing the e-book, be sure each image gallery displays the first image you want the reader to see.

Resizing and repositioning images

When you click an image in the gallery object, the Edit Mask panel appears near the gallery object, as shown in Figure 6-1. This panel works the same way as the Edit Mask controls described in Chapter 4: Use the slider to enlarge or shrink the image within its frame, and thus crop it.

You can reposition an image within its frame, as well. After clicking the image (to make the Edit Mask panel appear), click within the image and drag it to the desired position within its frame. Be sure you've selected the image and not the object; otherwise, you'll move the object itself, not the image within it.

You can't resize an image in a gallery beyond what the Edit Mask tool allows, so to fit an image larger than the current frame, you must resize the gallery object or use a program such as Adobe Photoshop to resize the image outside of iBooks Author. Then, add that resized version to your gallery, rather than the original image.

Changing image frames

You also can create curved corners around an image by selecting it and dragging the blue circle that appears near its upper-left corner sideways, as described in Chapter 4.

Deleting images

To delete an image, follow these steps:

1. **Select the image in the Gallery Media list in the Widget inspector's Interactive pane.**

   Or navigate to the desired image in the gallery object itself by using the left-arrow and right-arrow icon buttons.

2. **Press Delete.**

   You can also click the – (minus sign) icon button in the Interactive pane, press ⌘+X, choose Format➪Gallery➪Remove Image, choose Edit➪Cut, or choose Edit➪Delete.

   The image is deleted.

Setting gallery navigation controls

On an iPad, the reader simply swipes across an image to move among the images: Swiping left goes backward, and swiping right goes forward. Also by default, the reader sees an x of y indicator — such as 3 of 11 — below the image that notes which image (x) is currently displayed out of the total number of images (y) in that gallery.

But you can provide thumbnail navigation to the gallery, as shown in Figure 6-1: A row of image previews (called *thumbnails*) appears below the current image, and readers can tap a preview to jump to that image. To add the thumbnails, select the Show Thumbnails option in the Widget inspector's Interaction pane or choose

Format⇨Gallery⇨Show Image Thumbnails for Gallery. (If you show thumbnails, the *x* of *y* indicator is removed from the e-book's gallery.)

Whether readers navigate a gallery on the iPad by swiping or by tapping a preview, the current image's preview is highlighted with a yellow outline. If the number of previews doesn't fit in the gallery object, two or more dots appear below the thumbnails; each dot represents one gallery screen full of previews, and the dark dot represents the current set. The e-book's reader can tap a dot to jump to that screen's set of previews, and while the reader navigates through the images, the current set is highlighted.

Adjusting gallery captions

When you select each image in the gallery, double-click its caption to edit it. Each image has its own caption unless you choose Format⇨Gallery⇨Same Caption for All Images (in which case, the first image's caption is applied to all images). The gallery's title is the same for all images, and you can enter it no matter what image is displayed.

Interactive Images

A popular way to help people understand a diagram or elements in a photo on the web is to use rollovers, where a title and description appear when the pointer rolls over a certain spot. The interactive image widget object in iBooks Author has the same goal, though it works a bit differently. In iBooks Author, you can add titles and optional descriptions (together called *callouts* by publishers and *labels* by iBooks Author) to an image or diagram. When the e-book's reader taps the image or diagram, a detailed description is displayed, and the reader can zoom and/or move the focus of the image, such as to get a close-up view.

To add an Interactive Image widget, choose Interactive from the Widget icon menu in the toolbar or Insert⇨Widget⇨Interactive Image. After you add an interactive image object, you can add an image to it in a couple of ways:

- ✔ Drag an image from a folder or disk in the Finder onto the interactive image object.

- ✔ Select the image container inside the object — not the object itself — and paste a copied image into it. (To select the image container, click within its frame, not on some other part of the object.)

Either way, iBooks Author resizes the image to what it considers a good fit to the object's current size and opens the Widget inspector's Interaction pane. It also adds two placeholder callouts, as Figure 6-2 shows.

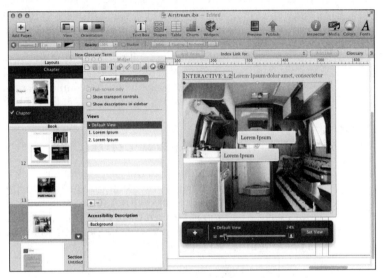

Figure 6-2: An interactive image object after adding an image to it.

Setting the default view

When you add an image to an interactive image object, or later select the image itself inside the object, the Set View panel appears. In this panel, you can

- ✔ Adjust its slider to zoom in or out of the image (similar to how you mask an image, as explained in Chapter 4 and in the section "Working with images," earlier in this chapter).

- ✔ Drag the image within its frame to crop it so that the desired portion appears for what the callout is describing; that crop is called the *focus*.

- ✔ Be sure that the panel indicates Default View at the top of the panel (see Figure 6-2), and then click Set View to save the image's zoom level and crop to what you just specified. This is how the image will appear when the reader opens the e-book and comes to this object.

If something other than your default view is selected, click Default View in the Interaction pane's Views list.

You can adjust the default view at any time by using the controls described in the preceding list.

You can have iBooks Author add navigation controls to all the selected interactive image object's views, which it calls *transport controls.* In the Widget inspector's Interaction pane, select the Show Transport Controls option or choose View⇨Interactive Image⇨Show Transport Controls.

On the iPad, the Back and Forward icon buttons (the left-pointing and right-pointing triangle icons, respectively) appear for the reader, as well as buttons for each image view that takes the reader to that specific view. (The order matches the order in the Views section of the Interaction pane, shown in Figure 6-2.) You see the same interface in iBooks Author, as shown in Figure 6-3, that the reader sees on the iPad.

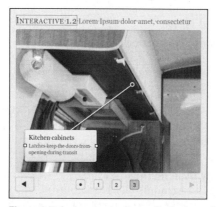

Figure 6-3: An interactive image's display, with the transport controls enabled.

Understanding image views

Each callout in an interactive image is its own view. You set the zoom and focus of each view separately, so when a reader taps a callout, the image's zoom and focus adjusts to what you set in iBooks Author. Typically, your default view is of the whole image, whereas each callout's view zooms into and focuses on an individual component. You don't have to change the view for each callout, but that's the intent behind this object's behavior.

To switch to a different view, choose View and then the view's name from the submenu that appears in the Interaction pane, or click the callout in the object. The title in the Set View panel changes accordingly. If you change a view's title (by double-clicking and editing it) you're changing its name, as well.

The e-book reader experiences the image in its default view. When the reader taps a callout, the image adjusts to match what you set for its view, and the callout expands to show its description, not just its title. The reader can also pan through the image by dragging the image but can't change the zoom level or rotate it. When the reader taps the callout, or anywhere else on the object, the image goes back to its default view.

Adding and setting image views

When you add an interactive image object, iBooks Author creates two image views, in addition to the main view, that both contain placeholder text.

Adding more image views

You can add additional image views in a few ways:

- ✔ Select the object and then click the + (plus sign) icon button in the Set View panel.
- ✔ Click the + (plus sign) icon button in the Views section of the Widget inspector's Interaction pane.
- ✔ Choose Format⇨Interactive Image⇨Add Label.

Delete an image view by selecting it in the Interaction pane's Views section and clicking the – (minus sign) icon button, or by selecting its callout in the object and choosing Format⇨Interactive Image⇨ Delete Label.

Editing image views' callout text

To change the callout's text, follow these steps:

1. **Double-click an image view's callout to make it editable.**

2. **Click the title and type in the text you want to use for the title.**

3. **(Optional) Click the description and type in the desired caption for it.**

   The text changes are saved automatically.

Setting the image views' zoom, focus, and callout position

Just like you set the zoom level and focus for the overall image in the default view (see the section "Setting the default view," earlier in this chapter), you also set the zoom level and focus of the image in each image view to change the image focus so that whatever the callout is describing is the center of the reader's attention. Often, you need to enlarge the image to show the specific portion of it that the callout describes.

The process for setting the image view's zoom level and focus is identical to setting these attributes for the default view (see the section "Setting the default view," earlier in this chapter), but you need to follow several additional steps for the image view that involve the position of the callouts and their callout lines:

1. **Go to the desired image view by clicking its callout.**

2. **In the View panel that appears, adjust the zoom level and focus of the image for the current callout so that the reader sees what's relevant to that callout.**

    You can make the following adjustments:

    • Adjust the slider to zoom in or out of the image (similar to how you mask an image, as explained in Chapter 4 and in the section "Working with images," earlier in this chapter).

    • Drag the image within its frame so the portion of the image that the callout describes appears (this process is setting the *focus*).

3. **Be sure that the top of the panel indicates Default View (see Figure 6-2), and then click Set View.**

    This step saves the image's zoom level and crops to what you specified in Step 2. The image will appear at this view when the reader taps its callout.

    You can change the image view later in the same way.

4. **To identify the center of the image view, drag the circle at the end of the callout line to where you want the image view's center to be.**

5. **Select the callout by clicking its edge, then drag it to the desired position so that it's visible.**

    You may need to zoom out to get to it, then zoom back in and set the image view again.

    If you can't see the callout in the image view, the e-book's reader won't see it there, either — just in the main view.

Figure 6-4 shows the image from Figure 6-2 with the callout repositioned, the callout line adjusted, and both the callout title (and thus the image view's name) and description modified for one of the image views.

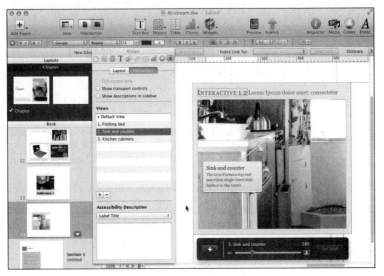

Figure 6-4: An image view with the callout, callout line, and callout title and description modified for the specific area of focus.

Adjusting callout display

Although the use of callouts with descriptions is the default presentation method for interactive images, you can have them appear in a translucent sidebar on the left side of the interactive image instead, as shown in Figure 6-5. You can do so in a couple of ways:

- ✔ Select the Show Descriptions in Sidebar option in the Widget inspector's Interaction pane.

- ✔ Choose Format➪Interactive Image➪Show Description in Sidebar.

This sidebar presentation for descriptions is handy when you have long descriptive text, but note that it does obscure quite a bit of your image, so you trade off image focus for text space. When this view is enabled, the callouts show only their titles, even when tapped; their descriptions appear in just the sidebar.

There's an additional aspect of the callout display to consider: Its accessibility descriptions. A visually impaired reader hears these descriptions spoken aloud when he navigates to the callout, assuming the iPad's VoiceOver feature is enabled. It's essentially the verbal display for the image view.

Figure 6-5: The optional sidebar view for descriptions.

In the Widget inspector's Interaction pane, the Accessibility Description pop-up menu (toward the bottom) has just one option for the default view: Background. Any text you enter in the field below is read aloud when the e-book's reader navigates to the interactive image's default view.

For each image view, the Accessibility Description pop-up menu has three options, one for each component of a callout: Label Title, Label Description, and Label Target. Choose each option in turn and enter the text in the field below for what's read aloud when the e-book reader navigates to, respectively, the callout title, the callout description, and the endpoint of the callout line (the label target).

3D Images

A very compelling capability in iBooks Author is its support of 3D objects that your e-book readers can rotate on their iPads. You need to create such a file in the Collada 3D model format (a `.dae` file) supported by programs such as Adobe Photoshop Extended (version CS5 or later), SketchUp, and Strata 3D.

To add a 3D image object to iBooks Author, choose 3D from the Widgets icon menu in the toolbar or choose Insert⇨Widget⇨3D.

You can get your Collada 3D file into the 3D image object in a couple of ways:

✔ Drag your file from the Finder onto the object.

✔ Import the file by clicking Choose in the Widget inspector's Interaction pane, navigating to the desired file in the settings sheet that appears, selecting that file, and clicking Insert.

If the 3D file is too complex to display on the iPad, a white field appears in the 3D image object. Otherwise, you get a static preview of the 3D image (you can't rotate it in iBooks Author), as Figure 6-6 shows.

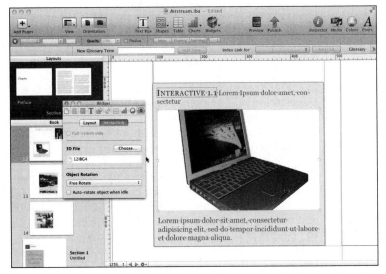
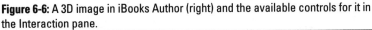

Figure 6-6: A 3D image in iBooks Author (right) and the available controls for it in the Interaction pane.

After you import the 3D file, you can use only two controls, available in both the Interaction pane and by choosing Format⇨3D:

✔ **Object Rotation pop-up menu:** You have three choices for how you want the image to rotate:

- *Free Rotate:* The default. Rotate the object in any direction along any axis.

- *Horizontal:* Spin the object around the *y* axis only (like a record on a record player).

- *Horizontal and Vertical:* Spin the object from side to side (along the *y* access) and up and down (along the *x* axis) — but not forward and back (along the *z* axis).

✔ **Auto-Rotate Object When Idle check box:** When this option is selected, the 3D object self-rotates when viewed on the iPad; enabling this option lets the e-book reader know the object is a 3D one that can be rotated by dragging.

Because you can't rotate a 3D object within iBooks Author, you should preview it in iBooks on an iPad (as explained in Chapter 2). Figure 6-7 shows two rotated views of the 3D object previewed in Figure 6-6 to show how rotation can appear.

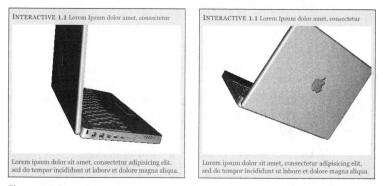

Figure 6-7: Two views of a rotated 3D object as displayed on an iPad.

Videos and Audio Files

Sometimes, the best way to present information is to show it in action or to hear someone talk about it. That's why the ability to include video and audio files in iBooks Author's movie object is so powerful.

To add a movie object, choose Movie in the Widgets icon menu in the toolbar or choose Insert➪Widget➪Movie. After you add the movie object, you add media files through the Media Browser panel. Those files need to be in a compatible format *and* available in one of Apple's media-savvy apps (GarageBand, iTunes, iPhoto, or iMovie) or, for video files only, in the Mac's Movies folder. Chapter 4 explains how to convert video and audio files to a supported format, how to make them accessible to iBooks Author, and how to use the Media Browser.

Figure 6-8 shows two movie objects, one of a video file and one of an audio file. The figure also shows how they appear in an e-book on the iPad.

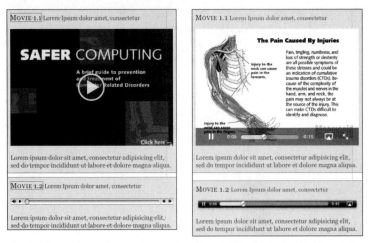

Figure 6-8: A video object and an audio object in iBooks Author (left), and the same objects in an e-book on the iPad (right).

The Interactive pane has a handful of controls available on movie objects:

- ✔ **Start & Stop:** Use the two scrub heads to change where the video or audio file starts (the left scrub head) and stops (the right scrub head). By default, the entire file plays.

- ✔ **Poster Frame:** Use this slider to pick the preview image (called a *poster*) for a video; while you slide through the video, you see the frame for where the slider is, and that frame becomes the preview image shown in the e-book for the video. Audio files have no preview image, so the slider is inactive.

- ✔ **Repeat:** This pop-up menu has two options: None and Loop. If you choose Loop, the video plays continuously in the e-book after the reader taps it to begin the playback. (You can also choose Format➪Media➪Loop to enable or disable looping.)

- ✔ **Controls:** These icon buttons let you go to the beginning, fast-forward, playback or pause, rewind, and go to the end of the select video or audio file, so you can check out the content and verify any adjustments you make to the start and stop positions. (These controls have no effect on the e-book itself; movie objects in the e-book display their own playback controls, as shown in Figure 6-8, after the reader taps the object.)

You can also just click a video to begin playback in iBooks Author; for audio, you can use the control bar that appears in the object (see Figure 6-8), rather than the controls in the Widget inspector's Interaction pane.

Keynote Presentations

Slideshows are a time-honored presentation method in meetings, so why not include them in an e-book? That's the thinking behind iBooks Author's support for them. Keynote is Apple's slideshow editor, and only slideshows in the Keynote format can be added to an iBooks Author e-book.

Apple's Keynote program can open Microsoft PowerPoint slideshows and save them to the Keynote format, so you can use PowerPoint slideshows in iBooks Author if you convert them to Keynote format.

To add a Keynote object, choose Keynote in the Widgets icon menu in the toolbar or choose Insert⇨Widget⇨Keynote. After you add the Keynote object, you can add a presentation to it by dragging a Keynote file from the Finder onto the object, or you can click Choose in the Widget inspector's Interaction pane, navigate to the desired file in the settings sheet that appears, select that file, and click Insert.

The Choose button doesn't work in iBooks Author 1.01 or earlier. So you have to drag the files in from the Finder instead. But it does work in iBooks Author 1.1 and later.

The iPad's iBooks app can handle most of what you can put in a Keynote presentation: hyperlinks, transition effects, videos, and the like. But readers can't access presenter notes, and iBooks doesn't support voiceover narration or autoplay features.

Figure 6-9 shows a Keynote object in iBooks Author; the display in an e-book is the same, with the only difference being that you can actually play a Keynote presentation in the e-book (tap it to start), whereas in iBooks Author, you can see only the initial slide.

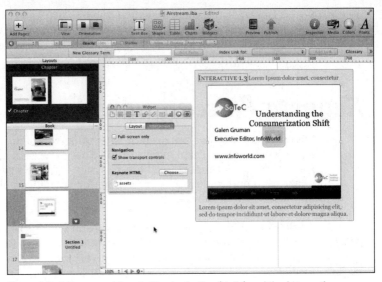

Figure 6-9: A Keynote object in iBooks Author (right) and the Interaction pane (center).

When you add a Keynote presentation, be sure to make its object's size appropriate for the presentation's content; the reader needs to be able to read the slideshow's text and see its elements clearly, after all!

When you select a Keynote object, just two options appear for it, both in the Widget inspector's Interaction pane:

✔ **Full-Screen Only:** Select this option to force the Keynote presentation to take over the iPad's screen when its object is tapped and play the presentation in full-screen mode. Enabling this option also changes the appearance of the Keynote object to a small preview, similar to what you get in portrait orientation (see Chapter 2).

✔ **Show Transport Controls:** Select this option (or choose Format➪Keynote➪Show Transport Controls) to display a bar at the bottom of the Keynote presentation, as shown in Figure 6-9, that lets the reader navigate the slides on the iPad.

Without the playback (transport) controls visible, a reader can tap the displayed slide to advance to the next slide. But with the playback controls visible, a reader can also go backwards or to the beginning of the slideshow.

Review Quizzes

iBooks Author was designed mainly for textbook creation, although you can use it for all sorts of books. As any student knows, textbooks typically have chapter review questions to test what the student has learned from that chapter. iBooks Author lets you add such chapter reviews to your e-books, with the twist that the student sees her score immediately.

You're not limited to just simple multiple-choice questions, either. You can present the multiple-choice questions in any of several sophisticated ways, which you determine independently for each question. For example, you can show a grid of images and have readers choose the correct one, or show an image and have readers move its labels to the correct positions on the image. Figure 6-10 shows three of the six review format options.

Although it's intended for chapter reviews, the review object is just as handy for adding quizzes of all sorts into an e-book.

To add a review object, choose Review in the Widgets icon menu in the toolbar or choose Insert⟹Widget⟹Review.

Setting questions and answers

A new review object has a standard list-style placeholder question with four placeholder possible answers, as Figure 6-11 shows. Of course, you can edit those questions and answers, but you can also choose among six types of questions and vary the number of questions. iBooks Author provides a lot of flexibility in how questions and their answers can be set up, as the following sections explain.

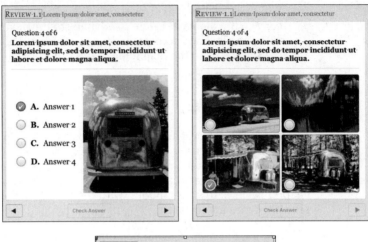

Figure 6-10: Three options for how review objects can present their questions: a list with image (top-left), an image grid (top-right), and a label-targeting exercise (bottom).

Adding questions

No matter what kind of questions you want to create for your review object, the basic process is the same. Follow these steps:

1. **Select the review object to which you want to add questions.**

2. **In the Widget inspector's Interaction pane, select a question whose contents and answers you want to change.**

3. **From the pop-up menu to the right of the selected question, choose the number of answers you're providing for that question.**

As Figure 6-11 shows, you can provide between two and six possible answers for any type of question.

The names of the questions in the Questions list match the question text you've entered in the review object, as Figure 6-11 shows.

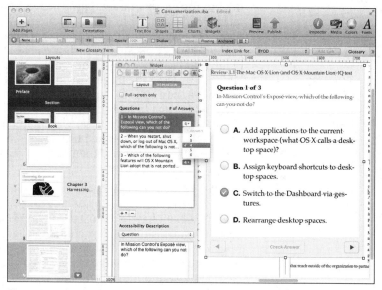

Figure 6-11: A review object with a simple list-style question (right) and the Interaction pane (center).

4. **(Optional) Click the + (plus sign) icon menu below the Questions list if you want to add a question, and then choose the question type that you want to add from the visual menu that appears, as shown in Figure 6-12.**

   You can also choose Format⇨Review⇨Add Question.

   Here's how the six kinds of questions work:

   • *Textual multiple choices:* The first three options, all labeled Multiple Choice, add questions that have a list of textual answers for the e-book's reader to choose from. The first option displays only text, whereas the other two options also add a graphics container into which you can drag or paste an image; Figure 6-10 shows one of the two possible layouts for such illustrated questions.

   You have the same Edit Mask control for the question's image that you do for any image, as detailed in Chapter 5.

- *Graphical multiple choice:* The fourth option, also labeled Multiple Choice, lets you create questions whose possible answers are all images — they can't have any text.

- *Identification labels:* The final two options provide label targets on an image for the e-book reader to drag to the correct target on the image. (Add the image by dragging it from the Finder or by pasting it.) If you choose the Drag Label to Target option, iBooks Author places a circular target for each of the number of answers assigned to this question, as shown in Figure 6-10. Drag the targets over whatever part of the image they refer to, and double-click their labels' placeholder text to add the label. At the bottom of the object, separate labels appear with matching text; in an e-book, a reader sees just the targets on the image and the labels below, and then has to drag the each label to the correct label.

The Drag Thumbnail to Target option works the same way, but instead of providing text labels that e-book readers have to drag to the proper targets, it provides small squares that contain images that the reader is supposed to drag to the correct target. (Add the images by dragging them from the Finder or by pasting them into the appropriate container.)

5. **Double-click a question's text in the review object to make that text editable.**

6. **Type or paste in the desired text.**

Editing multiple-choice answers

Of course, adding the questions isn't enough. You also need to provide the possible answers and indicate which answers are correct for multiple-choice questions. Follow these steps:

1. **Select the review object.**

2. **In the Widget inspector's Interactive pane, select the question whose answers you want to edit.**

3a. **For a question with text answers, double-click the text in the review object, and then type in or paste in the desired answer.**

3b. **For graphical multiple-choice questions, drag from the Finder or paste into each image's frame the desired image for that answer.**

4. **Repeat the appropriate Step 3 for each answer.**

5. **Click the correct answer's selection bubble in the review object.**

   A green check mark appears on its selection bubble. To select more than one correct answer, Shift-click the other correct answers.

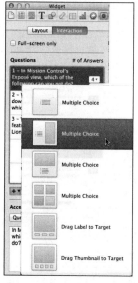

Figure 6-12: The icon menu's options for adding questions to a review.

For identification-label questions, you don't indicate the correct answer because the reader doesn't choose from a set of questions, but instead has to drag the correct label to the correct portion of the image, as described in the preceding section. That nature of identification-label questions also explains why you can't have multiple correct answers; each label corresponds to one and only one part of the image.

Reordering questions

To reorder the questions, select one in the Questions list, and then drag it to a new location in the list.

You can't reorder answers the way you reorder questions. Instead, you must edit the answers to have them appear in the desired order.

Deleting questions

To delete an unwanted question, select it in the Interaction pane and click the – (minus sign) icon button or choose Format⊅ Review⊅Remove Question.

Controlling review display

Select the Full-Screen Only option in the Widget inspector's Interaction pane to force the selected review object to appear in full-screen mode on the iPad.

Enabling this option also changes the appearance of the review object on the iPad and in iBooks Author to a small preview, similar to what you get in portrait orientation (see Chapter 2). On the iPad, when the reader taps the review object on the iPad, the review object expands to take over the iPad's entire screen. When the reader has completed the review, the review object shrinks back into its preview size in the e-book.

Taking a quiz

Although this book is about creating e-books in iBooks Author, not using the iBooks e-reader on the iPad, you need to know how review quizzes actually work in iBooks if you want to create effective ones in your iBooks Author e-books. The way to take a quiz isn't intuitive, so you may want to give readers explicit instructions in your review object's caption.

Follow these steps to take a quiz on the iPad:

1. **Tap a review object to begin the quiz.**

   The first question and its possible answers (for a multiple-choice question) appear.

2. **For a multiple-choice question, tap the selection bubble for the answer you believe is correct.**

   A black check mark indicates your selection.

   If it's an identification-label quiz, drag the labels to the targets believed to be correct.

3. **Tap the Check Answer button to register your answer.**

   If the answer is wrong, the selected answer displays a white X in a red background, and you can try again — again, tapping Check Answer to register the new answer.

   If you tap the Next icon button (the right-facing triangle) to move onto the next question without tapping Check Answer, the e-book doesn't check the answer's accuracy when it provides the score at the end of the quiz and thus counts it as a wrong answer.

4. After you check the question's answer, tap Next.

You proceed to the next question.

5. Repeat Steps 2 through 4 for each question.

6. (Optional) Go back through questions by tapping the Previous icon button (shown as a left-facing triangle) to change your previous answers.

This approach means that iBooks Author quizzes aren't meant so much for game-style quizzes but as a way to test readers in a way that helps them discover the correct answer along the way.

When you finish the quiz, the e-book shows the number of correct answers and explains that you can go back and adjust any answers, as desired, or tap the Start Over button to clear the check marks from the answers you selected. (Closing the e-book by going back to the iBooks Library also clears the answers you selected.)

Web Widgets

For the ambitious e-book developer, iBooks Author provides HTML objects that can contain HTML snippets (what Apple calls web widgets), which let you run website-like functionality from an e-book. You can't just copy the HTML code for a standard web page, however — you have to create what Apple calls a web widget by using its Dashcode tool, a free download from the Apple website (it does require that you register as a developer): `http://developer.apple.com/downloads`. Dashcode is the tool that you use to create widgets for the Safari browser and for Mac OS X's Dashboard — and now for iBooks Author's HTML objects. There are also third-party tools that you can use to create Dashcode widgets, such as Tumult's Hype 1.5.

Dashcode is very template-driven, so you pick the type of Dashboard widget you want to create and then follow the steps that Dashcode indicates to create the widget through a mix of HTML code, Cascading Style Sheets (CSS), and JavaScript code. This guided-template approach means you don't need to be a web developer to create several kinds of web widgets in Dashcode.

But the ins and outs of creating a web widget in Dashcode can quickly go beyond what most iBooks Author users will do and can easily require deeper knowledge of HTML programming, so I recommend you get Apple's Dashcode manual by going to `http://developer.apple.com` and searching for *Dashcode User Guide*. Also, several aspects of a Dashcode widget are allowed for Mac OS X widgets, but not for iBooks Author HTML objects; Apple details these differences in a support document at `http://support.apple.com/kb/HT5068`.

Options in iBooks Author

Before I get into the basics of using Dashcode (see the following section), you should know how HTML objects work in both iBooks Author and in the e-book when read on the iPad's iBooks app.

When you do have an HTML object in iBooks Author, it doesn't have any controls beyond the standard formatting options for any object container, as explained in Chapter 4.

To add an HTML object, choose HTML in the Widgets icon menu in the toolbar or choose Insert⇨Widget⇨HTML. To get the web widget code into a selected HTML object, you have a couple of options:

- ✔ Drag the Dashcode widget file from the Finder onto the object.

- ✔ Click Choose in the Widget inspector's Interaction pane to open a settings sheet, where you can locate a Dashcode file, select it, and then click Insert to add it to the HTML object. Figure 6-13 shows an HTML object and the Interaction pane for the inspector's Widget pane.

If your web widget uses a disallowed capability (detailed at `http://support.apple.com/kb/HT5068`), iBooks Author displays an alert that explains the incompatibility, and your web widget isn't imported. After you fix the issue in Dashcode, you can import or drag the widget file in again. But you may still get the error message, even if there's no longer an incompatibility; in that case, quit iBooks Author and reopen it to clear iBooks Author's memory of the original error so that it can assess the revised widget's compatibility cleanly.

Although you can resize the object, the only thing that appears in the object itself are a graphic representing the web widget (the preview image, which is also called the *poster image*), the title, caption, and container. After the reader taps the HTML object on the iPad, the rest of the book disappears, and the web widget takes over the screen until the reader closes it.

You can change the preview image for the HTML object by dragging a new graphic over the HTML object's existing graphic; this action replaces the preview image in iBooks Author but not in the original Dashcode widget file.

 Because HTML objects play back in full-screen mode on the iPad, the default size for an HTML object is relatively small, under the assumption that the preview image is more like a button or an icon than a detailed facsimile of a web page. You can resize the HTML object like any other object if your preview image warrants a larger size.

When you're working in iBooks Author, you can run the web widget on your Mac by following these steps:

1. **Click the Edit HTML floating button that appears beneath the HTML object when you select it (see Figure 6-13).**

   Despite the button's name, you can't edit the HTML code in iBooks Author.

   The web widget runs.

2. **When you're done, click the Done floating button.**

   Alternatively, you can press Esc.

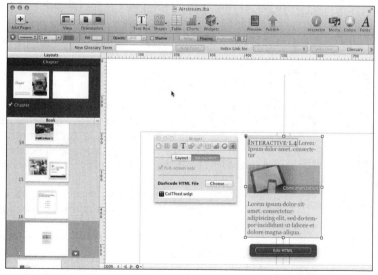

Figure 6-13: An HTML object (right) and the Widget inspector's Interaction pane (center).

To edit your web widget, go to Dashcode, save a new version of the widget file, and import or drag the new version into its HTML object in iBooks Author.

Creating a Dashcode widget

If you plan on doing more than basic Dashcode widgets, you need solid HTML, CSS, and JavaScript skills. But the basic process for creating a web widget is the same, regardless of its complexity.

Choosing the web widget type

When creating a web widget in Dashcode, the first decision is the type of web widget you want to create. To specify the widget type, follow these steps:

1. **Launch the Dashcode application on your Mac.**

2. **Open a new project by choosing File⇨New Project.**

   Alternatively, you can press ⌘+N.

3. **Choose Dashboard as the widget type from the left pane in the settings sheet that appears (see Figure 6-14).**

   You can't use Safari widgets in iBooks Author.

4. **Select the desired template from the settings sheet, and then click Choose.**

   You can also click Open Existing to continue working on a previously created widget.

Designing the web widget

In the project window that opens after you create a widget (see the preceding section), a list of object attributes appears in the left pane, and a list of tasks appears at the bottom of that pane. The options vary based on the type of widget you chose to create; Figure 6-15 shows the attributes for an RSS-reading widget.

More-complex widgets can have multiple components — MPEG-4 (.m4v) video files, MPEG-4 (.m4a) audio files, buttons, graphics, lists, and much more. (Any iBooks Author e-book you distribute through the Apple iBookstore is protected so that readers can't copy its contents, but video and audio files in an HTML object aren't protected, so a reader can copy them.)

The Inspector in the center of the Dashcode project window in Figure 6-15 shows the attributes for the RSS feed's front window (the selected object in the left pane), which I've set to take the original iPad's and the iPad 2's full (1024-by-768-pixel) resolution.

Figure 6-14: The New Project settings sheet in Dashcode.

Figure 6-15: Setting the visual attributes of an RSS widget.

The third-generation iPad has a screen resolution of 2048 by 1536 pixels, but you still set the web widget's dimensions for the 1024-by-768-pixel resolution, both for compatibility with the millions of earlier-generation iPads and because the third-generation iPad uses its extra resolution not to cram more pixels on the screen but to produce smoother pixels that look more like real-life images.

Because web widgets in iBooks Author's HTML objects run at full screen on the iPad, take full advantage of that screen size for your widgets. Having a small widget floating in the iPad's full screen can look weird. Obviously, if the widget can't take advantage of the full screen, then don't use it all — but you can probably at least make an interesting background so that the widget looks nice in that full-screen display.

After you set the web widget's visuals, go through the various components listed at the bottom of the left pane. In Figure 6-16, these components are Widget Attributes, Default Image (what appears as the preview image in the HTML object in iBooks Author), and Widget Icon. You can also display (and edit) the relevant code below the main window by choosing View➪Source Code or pressing ⌘+2.

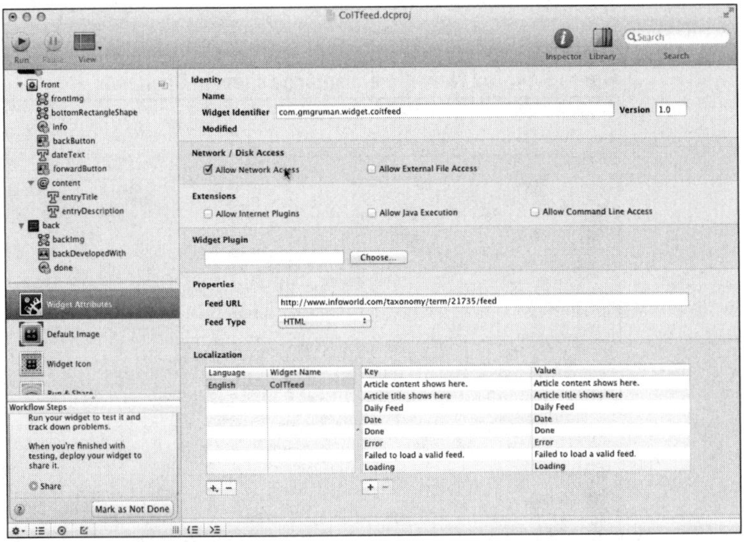

Figure 6-16: The attributes for the RSS widget.

Completing the workflow steps

Below the components list is the Workflow Steps pane, which lets you scroll through the steps needed to complete the web widget, with required actions listed. Click the triangle icon to a requirement's left to have the main window show the appropriate settings. (If the Workflow Steps pane doesn't appear, choose View➪Steps or press Option+⌘+3.) Click Mark as Done for each workflow step you've completed so that you can easily track your progress.

When setting a web widget's attributes, note the following:

✔ Give the web widget a unique name in the Widget Identifier field by changing the portion of the name after the `.widget.` portion of the name. You should also update the version number if you make a new version of the widget after releasing it to others. (There's no need to update the version number while you work on the first version of the widget and fix any issues before you distribute it publicly.)

✔ Be sure that the following attributes — all incompatible with the iPad — are *not* selected: Allow External File Access, Allow Internet Plugins, Allow Java Execution, and Allow Command Line Access. Also make sure no plugin name appears in the Widget Plugin field.

Preview your web widget by clicking the Run button in the toolbar.

Saving and exporting the web widget

To get the web widget into iBooks Author, go to the final workflow step (Test & Share) and click the Share option. Click Save to Disk to create the widget (`.wdgt`) file that can be imported or dragged into iBooks Author.

Clicking Deploy to Dashboard causes the web widget to be added to your Mac's Dashboard application, so you can run it on your Mac. After all, creating widgets to run on Macs was Dashcode's original purpose.

Choosing File⇨Save As doesn't create a widget file; it creates a project file, which can't be imported into iBooks Author. In other words, you work with the project file but create the widget file when you finish tweaking the project file so that you can use it in iBooks Author (and, optionally, your Mac's Dashboard).

Chapter 7

Working with E-Book Metadata

*W*hen information is digital, it can become both contextual and actionable. For example, e-books don't have an index in the way that printed books do because a reader simply has to search the e-book to find where a term is used — no longer must an editor seek every occurrence of a term that the reader might be expected to search for and compile the page number for each occurrence to build an index. (Traditional publishers may wail about the lack of an index, but it's just the way it is in e-books, whether produced in iBooks Author or another program.)

That type of information about information (in this case, the location of each occurrence of a term) is called *metadata,* which literally means "data about data." (Apple calls them *updating text fields.*)

You can take advantage of several kinds of metadata in an e-book, whether created in iBooks Author or some other tool. Some kinds of metadata, such as cross-references within the book, are much easier to create in iBooks Author than in the tools typically used by publishers to create regular e-books. And iBooks Author also adds a unique form of metadata to its e-books: glossaries.

So, what are the types of metadata you can take advantage of in iBooks Author? They are

✔ Document metadata (such as author and keyword information)

✔ Chapter titles

✔ Page numbering

✔ Cross-references

✔ Bookmarks

✔ Hyperlinks to web resources

✔ Tables of contents

✔ Glossaries

Setting Document Metadata

You can set a few descriptors for an iBooks Author e-book in the Document inspector's Document pane, shown in Figure 7-1, to help readers find the e-book more easily via their Macs' Spotlight search function (for those free e-books not distributed via the iBookstore): author name, e-book title, and keywords (separated by commas).

For e-books published to the iBookstore, you enter the document metadata in Apple's iTunes Producer application. (See Chapter 8 for more about this application and distributing your e-book.)

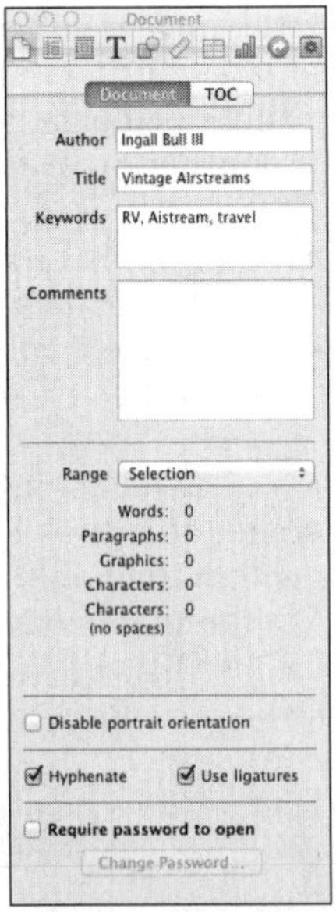

Figure 7-1: The Document inspector's Document pane.

Using Chapter and Section Titles

When you create chapters, the opening page shows Untitled as its title or — for chapters imported from Microsoft Word or Apple Pages — the filename of the imported file. You probably want a more descriptive title. To give a chapter a title, follow these steps:

1. **In the Book panel, Control-click (or right-click) that chapter to open a contextual menu.**

   Chapter 2 explains the Book panel, which is always open at the left side of the iBooks Author application window.

2. **Choose Rename from the contextual menu (as shown in Figure 7-2).**

   The chapter's name is now selected, so you can edit it.

3. **Enter the desired title.**

   The new title is automatically reflected in that chapter's opener.

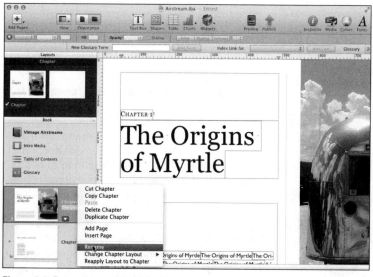

Figure 7-2: Renaming a chapter's title.

You change a section's title by following the preceding steps, except you Control-click or right-click the section title, rather than the chapter title, to select it so that you can enter the new title.

But what makes that title appear in the chapter opener? By default, in the layout that the chapter is based on, the text box that contains the placeholder chapter title (Chapter) has metadata inserted that tells iBooks Author to substitute the current chapter name for that metadata's placeholder text. Likewise, a section opener's title is typically set as metadata, and so are the chapter and section numbers.

Inserting chapter and section metadata

You can insert metadata into any text, not just the text boxes set up for you by the iBooks Author template. Just follow these steps:

1. **Place the text cursor at the desired location in a text box.**

2. **Choose Insert⇨Section Title.**

   The type of layout determines what replaces the metadata:

   - *Chapter layout:* The chapter name in a chapter opener and in any text boxes that use it in that layout's subsequent pages

   - *Section layout:* The section name in a section opener and in any text boxes that use it in that layout's subsequent pages

   - *Page layout:* The book name in whatever text box has that metadata

Related metadata are the chapter and section numbers. To add them to text, place the text cursor at the desired location and choose Insert⇨Section Number. While you add, delete, and rearrange chapters and sections, iBooks Author renumbers these references automatically wherever they're used.

 These metadata are also handy for use in folios, the headers and footers that often appear at the top of a layout's pages to display the current chapter or section name and/or number, in addition to the current page number (as explained in the section "Applying page numbering," later in this chapter).

Setting chapter and section metadata display options

You can change what text the metadata displays. Follow these steps:

1. **Go to the text box in the layout that contains the metadata and select that metadata.**

   Don't select just its text box.

2. **Control-click (or right-click) the metadata and choose Book (for the book title), Chapter (for the chapter title), or Section (for the section title) from the contextual menu that appears.**

   You can also double-click the selected metadata to open a panel whose pop-up menu provides the same choices. *Note:* For chapter layouts' metadata, your only options are Book and Chapter.

If you want to change the metadata setting for a specific page in the document, select the metadata and choose the desired option. Only that one instance of the metadata is affected.

Likewise, you can change how chapter and section labels appear by following these steps:

1. **Select the metadata whose label you want to change.**

2. **Control-click (or right-click) the metadata to open a contextual menu.**

   Alternatively, you can double-click the selected metadata to open a panel that displays the options that appear in the contextual menu.

3. **Choose the desired display option.**

   You can choose Prefix and Number, Prefix Only, or Number Only. *Prefix* means Chapter or Section. Figure 7-3 shows both the contextual menu and the panel that contain these options.

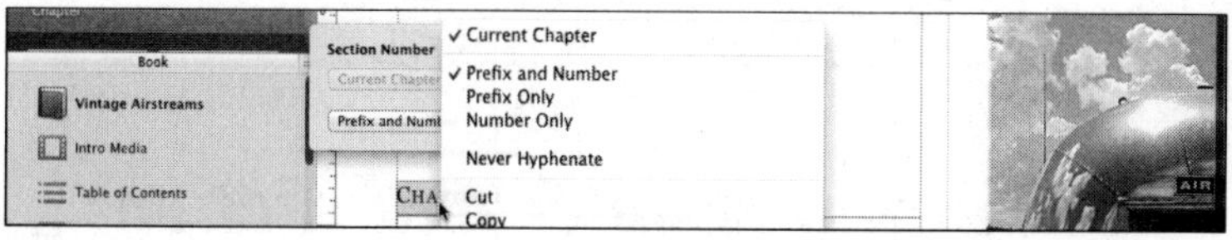

Figure 7-3: Altering the display of a chapter or section number in its label.

Also, you can change the presentation of the numbers themselves. By default, chapter and section numbers are presented as numerals (1, 2, 3, and so on), but you can also have iBooks Author use Roman numerals (I, II, III, and so on) or letters (A, B, C, and so on). Follow these steps:

1. **In the Layout inspector, go to the Numbering pane, shown in Figure 7-4, by clicking its label.**

2a. **To change the numbering presentation for all chapters (or sections) based on a specific layout, first select those chapters' (or sections') layout in the Layouts panel and then, in the Layout inspector's Numbering pane, choose the desired option from the Format pop-up menu in the Section Numbers section.**

   The options are 1,2,3; a,b,c; A,B,C; i,ii,iii; and I,II,III.

   If the Layouts panel doesn't appear above the Pages panel, choose View⇨Show Layouts to display it.

2b. **To change a specific chapter's (or section's) numbering presentation, first select that chapter's (or section's) opener in the Book panel and then, in the Layout inspector's Numbering pane, choose the desired option from the Format pop-up menu in the Section Numbers section.**

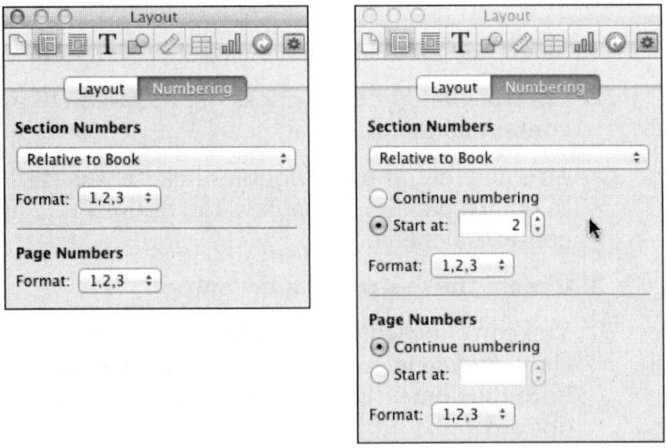

Figure 7-4: The Layout inspector's Numbering pane when in a chapter or section layout (left) and when in a document page (right).

Setting chapter and section numbering options

You can also set for specific chapters and sections how their chapter or section numbers are determined:

1. **In the Book panel, select the chapter opener or section opener whose numbering you want to specify.**

2. **Make a selection from the pop-up menu at the top of the Section Numbers section.**

   The menu has two options for chapters' layouts and document pages (for sections' layouts and pages based on them, it has an additional option):

   - *Relative to Book:* The chapter's or section's number is based on how many chapters or sections appeared before it in the book. Thus, if the current section is in the ninth one in the book, its number is 9, regardless of the chapter it's in. If you choose Relative to Chapter (for a section layout or page), the section numbers start anew at each chapter, so if that ninth section in the book is the first section in the current chapter, its number is 1.

   - *None:* iBooks Author inserts the chapter or section title, rather than its number; if you select this option, you may end up with doubled use of the title if the metadata for the chapter's or section's number is set to display both its title and number, resulting in something like THE ORIGINS OF MYRTLE The Origins of Myrtle.

   - *Relative to Chapter:* Available only for section layouts and their pages, this option works like Relative to Book, except that it affects just the section numbers. In each chapter, the section numbering begins at 1 if you choose this option, instead of following from the previous chapter's last section number.

3. **(Optional) In the Layout inspector's Numbering pane, select Start At in the Section Numbers section (see Figure 7-4) and enter the desired number in the adjacent field.**

   Alternatively, you can use the stepper controls to adjust this value.

   That section's number is now the one you entered, regardless of whether that number matches its sequence in the book.

   The default option is Continue Numbering, in which the current chapter or section uses the next number in the book's sequence. For example, if the previous chapter was the third chapter, the current chapter is numbered 4 if Continue Numbering is selected.

4. **(Optional) In the Layout inspector's Numbering pane, select Start At in the Page Numbers section and enter the desired number in the adjacent field.**

Alternatively, use the stepper controls to adjust this value.

The first page in that section now starts with the number you entered, regardless of whether that matches its sequence in the book.

If you leave the default option, Continue Numbering, the current chapter or section uses the next page number in the book's sequence. For example, if you don't change this setting from the default, if the previous chapter ended on page 45, the current chapter's first page is 46.

Applying Page Numbering

iBooks Author can automatically insert page numbers in folios and other text locations. To insert that metadata, place the text cursor in the box at the location where you want the page number to appear, and then choose Insert⇨Page Number.

If you use the page number metadata in a text box in a layout, all chapters or sections based on that layout have that text box and its page number metadata, which thus ensures that each page based on that layout are automatically numbered. (The preceding section explains how to change the starting page number for sections and chapters.)

A related option is the metadata for the total page count, which appears in text such as Page x of y). Place the text cursor in the text box location where you want this metadata to appear, then choose Insert⇨Page Count to enter the total number of pages in the e-book.

For both page numbers and page counts, iBooks Author keeps the numbers updated automatically while you add and delete pages in the e-book.

Using Cross-References and Hyperlinks

The hyperlink, another form of metadata, makes a text selection into a tappable item that can then open a web page in the iPad's Safari browser, begin an e-mail message in its Mail app, or jump to another part of the current e-book (meaning a hyperlink can be a cross-reference).

Working with cross-references

You can add bookmarks to specific text locations, providing a destination for a cross-reference hyperlink. When you create an object that has a title (see Chapter 5), such a bookmark is automatically created.

To add a bookmark, follow these steps:

1. **Insert the text cursor in a text box or shape on any document page — except a chapter or section opener.**

   Alternatively, select a word or phrase in a text box or shape.

   You can't create a hyperlink from text in a figure caption.

   I suggest you select a word or phrase so that you can more easily find the bookmark location later; the bookmarked text has a blue frame placed around it (this frame doesn't appear to the reader in the e-book on the iPad).

2. **Choose Insert⇨Bookmark.**

   The Hyperlink inspector's Bookmark pane appears, listing the bookmark and its page number. If you selected a word or phrase when creating the bookmark, that text appears as the bookmark's name; otherwise, the word Bookmark is used.

3. **Double-click the bookmark's name to make it editable, and then enter the name you want to use.**

To create a cross-reference to a bookmark you created, follow these steps:

1. **Go to a location in the book that you want e-book readers to be able to tap to get to that bookmarked location.**

2. **Select the text that the reader should tap.**

3. **Choose Insert⇨Hyperlink⇨Bookmark.**

   The Hyperlink inspector's Hyperlink pane opens.

4. **Choose the destination bookmark from the Name pop-up menu.**

You can also create a cross-reference by following these steps:

1. **Select the text that you want to act as the hyperlink.**

2. **Go to the Hyperlink inspector's Hyperlink pane.**

3. **Select the Enable as Hyperlink option.**

4. **Choose Bookmark from the Link To pop-up menu.**

5. **Choose the destination bookmark from the Name pop-up menu.**

Why would you choose one method over the other? Personal preference, mainly. The first method is for those people who like to work with menus, and the second is for those who like to work in panels. The second method can be more efficient, especially if you're adding multiple hyperlinks, because the Hyperlinks inspector stays open until you close it and because you don't have to keep going back to the menu.

After you add the hyperlink, the *origin text* (what the reader taps to jump to the destination bookmark) is highlighted with a blue rectangle (which isn't visible in the e-book on the iPad) and styled as blue underlined text (which is retained in the iPad's e-book so that readers know the text is a hyperlink). Figure 7-5 shows the Hyperlink inspector's Hyperlink and Bookmark panes.

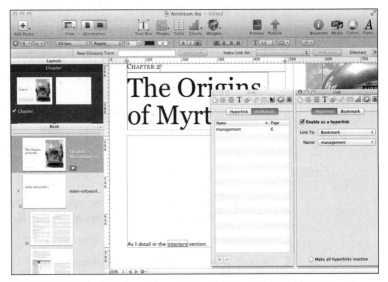

Figure 7-5: The Bookmark and Hyperlink panes, as well as text (styled as blue and underlined) that's been made into a hyperlink.

To create a cross-reference to a *figure* (an object that has a title, as described in Chapter 5), follow these steps:

1. **Select the text that you want to make into a hyperlink.**

2. Choose Insert⇨Hyperlink⇨Figure Reference to open the Hyperlink inspector's Hyperlink pane.

   You can also go directly to that pane and select the Enable as Hyperlink option.

3. Choose Figure in the Link To pop-up menu to create a cross-reference to a figure.

4. In the In pop-up menu, specify the locations to which you want to limit the figure entries in the Name list at the bottom of the pane.

   The options are Current Chapter, Entire Book, and the titles of each chapter and section in the book. If you choose anything other than Entire Book, only figures in that chosen part of the book appear in the Name list.

5. In the Style pop-up menu, choose a style of figure to which you want to limit the Name list entries.

   The options are All Figure Styles, Diagram, Figure, Gallery, Image, Illustration, Interactive, Movie, and Review. (You set the figure style in the Label pop-up menu in the Widget inspector's Layout pane, as explained in Chapter 5.)

6. In the Name list, which shows all figures that match the criteria set in the In and Style pop-up menus, select the desired figure.

   The cross-reference to that figure is applied to the selected text, which is now a hyperlink to that figure.

Text that has a figure cross-reference applied also has the character Style Figure Reference applied to it automatically, which makes the text medium-blue and underlined.

Working with web and e-mail hyperlinks

The process to create hyperlinks to web addresses and e-mail addresses is similar to the process for creating cross-references described in the preceding section. Just follow these steps:

1. Select the text to which you want to apply the hyperlink.

2. Choose Insert⇨Webpage or Insert⇨Email Message, as appropriate.

   The Hyperlink inspector's Hyperlink pane appears.

3. **In the Hyperlink pane, fill in the destination information.**

   For a web page, enter the web address in the URL field. For an e-mail message, enter the destination address in the To field and, optionally, a predefined e-mail subject line in the Subject field.

Text that has such hyperlinks applied has the character style Hyperlink applied automatically, which by default makes the origin text red.

Editing hyperlinks

You can edit and format the *origin text* (the tappable hyperlink that the reader sees in the e-book) just like you can any other text in the e-book, as Chapter 3 details.

To select hyperlinked text, follow these steps:

1. **Insert the text cursor somewhere other than the hyperlinked text.**

2. **Use the arrow keys to move the cursor immediately next to the hyperlinked text.**

3. **Hold Shift and press the appropriate arrow keys to select the rest of the hyperlinked text.**

4. **Release the Shift key when done.**

You select hyperlinked text as described in the preceding steps because clicking within the hyperlinked text makes iBooks Author execute the hyperlink, opening a web page, opening your e-mail program, or having your page change.

To change a hyperlink, select the origin text and adjust the options in the Hyperlink pane. You can, for example, change the hyperlink type (such as from Web Page to Figure) or the destination (the URL, e-mail address, bookmark, or figure).

Removing and disabling hyperlinks

You may have added hyperlinks or bookmarks at an earlier time that you no longer want to have in the document. And you may want to retain the hyperlinks but make them temporarily inactive so that you don't accidentally click them in iBooks Author to jump elsewhere in the book, or open a web page or e-mail. iBooks Author has a way to handle each of these scenarios:

- ✔ **Disable hyperlinks.** If you're doing substantial work in the e-book document in iBooks Author, you can disable all hyperlinks to prevent such unwanted hyperlink launches. Just select the Make All Hyperlinks Inactive check box in the Hyperlink inspector's Hyperlink pane. When you deselect the option, the hyperlinks all work again.

- ✔ **Remove a hyperlink from text.** Select that text, go to the Hyperlink pane and deselect Enable as Hyperlink. After you remove the hyperlink, selecting Enable as Hyperlink again does *not* restore the original hyperlink; instead, you have to enter the hyperlink again.

The automatic hyperlink formatting applied by iBooks Author isn't removed when you disable a hyperlink, so you need to undo that formatting yourself. To do so, select the text and apply the None character style.

- ✔ **Remove a bookmark.** This process removes a bookmark that you created, not a figure bookmark. Go to the Hyperlink inspector's Bookmark pane, select the bookmark that you want to remove, and click the – (minus sign) icon button. The hyperlink to that bookmark is also removed, but not its text formatting. (See the section "Working with cross-references," earlier in this chapter, for details on creating the bookmarks used in cross-references.)

Creating Tables of Contents

iBooks Author creates a table of contents (TOC) for your book automatically. You tell iBooks Author which paragraph styles' text should be used to create the TOC, and it builds the TOC automatically, keeping it updated while you work on your e-book.

The Document inspector's TOC pane is where you determine what text is used to create the TOC. By default, all paragraph styles that include the word Heading are used, as is the paragraph style Title. Select a paragraph style and click the – (minus sign) icon button to remove a paragraph style and thus any text using it from the TOC. Click the + (plus sign) icon menu to add a paragraph style to the TOC-creation list; in the menu that appears, select the specific paragraph style that you want to add to the TOC.

Also included in the TOC-creation list are three predefined section layouts in the e-book that you may have used to create pages — Copyright, Dedication, and Foreword — as well as all sections in the e-book. You can remove any of these pages or sections from the TOC by selecting them in the TOC pane and clicking the – (minus sign) icon button.

To open the TOC when reading the e-book in iBooks, the reader taps the iPad's screen to display the iBooks controls, and then taps the TOC icon button (it looks like a three-line bulleted list) at the top. (If the book also has a glossary, the reader then needs to tap the Table of Contents button that appears, rather than the TOC icon button; the Glossary button also appears if the book has a glossary.) What the reader then sees depends on the e-book's orientation:

✔ **Landscape orientation:** Displays a TOC for each chapter; the reader navigates through the chapter's page thumbnails at the bottom of the screen (they appear after the reader taps the screen). Tapping a title jumps the reader to the text that has that heading, and tapping a thumbnail page jumps to that page. In iBooks Author, a similar view appears by double-clicking the Table of Contents item in the Book panel. You can edit, format, resize, and move the elementsin the TOC like you can objects in any other layout (see Chapter 4), except that you can't add widgets.

✔ **Portrait orientation:** The reader sees a simple list of all the chapters and their headings for the entire book. The down-pointing caret character to the right of a chapter name is an icon button that the reader can tap to display all the headings in that chapter. When the headings are displayed, the icon button turns into an up-pointing caret, which the reader taps to close the headings list. You see essentially the same thing in iBooks Author. The only thing you can change in the portrait orientation's TOC in iBooks Author is the book title at the very top, which you can edit and format.

In both orientations, you can have iBooks Author display the page numbers for the titles and headings. To do so, select the Show Page Numbers in TOC option in the Document inspector's TOC pane.

Creating Glossaries

One of the nicer advances in e-books brought by iBooks Author is its glossary capability. A *glossary* is a list of terms with definitions — essentially, a custom mini-dictionary at the end of a book. iBooks Author makes it easy to create a glossary for your e-book, but it also does something nice for the readers: It lets them click glossary terms in the book's text and jump to the definition, applying a hyperlink from the term to the glossary item.

You don't need to add a glossary to your e-book. iBooks Author omits the glossary entirely if you define no glossary terms, so you don't have to worry about a blank glossary appearing in your e-book.

Adding glossary items

The simplest way to work with adding glossary items to have the Glossary bar open. Follow these steps to add items by using the Glossary bar:

1. **Choose View⇨Show Glossary Bar.**

   Alternatively, you can press Shift+⌘+E.

   The Glossary bar appears beneath the Format bar (which, if open, appears below the toolbar).

2. **While you go through the text, select a term when you come across it.**

   When you select a term, it appears in the Glossary bar's New Glossary Term field.

3. **Click the Add Glossary Term button to the right of the New Glossary Term field.**

   Or you can choose Format⇨Create Glossary Term from Selection or press Option+⌘+E.

   The term is boldfaced in your text (meaning it's the primary occurrence of that term) and added to the e-book's glossary. (I explain how to add the term's definition in the section "Adding glossary terms' definitions," later in this chapter.)

   The term also becomes tappable in the iPad and clickable in iBooks Author (like a hyperlink), and tapping or clicking it opens the glossary's definition for the term.

You can also add terms from the glossary itself by clicking the + (plus sign) icon button in the glossary's Glossary pane (which I explain in the section "Adding glossary terms' definitions," later in this chapter). However, you can't apply such terms to text in the e-book itself as the primary term, only as index links.

Tips when adding glossary links

After you add a term to the glossary in the e-book, you can't remove that primary glossary link later on — for example, you can't move the link to a different occurrence of the term. So be sure you add the primary glossary link by using the occurrence of the term that you want to highlight in boldface to indicate a glossary entry.

Add terms to the glossary after you finish editing the e-book so that you don't miss a term for use as a primary glossary link nor its later occurrences for use as index terms.

Adding index links

Traditionally, you add the first occurrence of a term to the glossary as the primary glossary link, under the assumption that people read your book from start to finish. But what if the reader didn't read the term in its first occurrence? Or if the reader saw the term but didn't click it to look up the meaning?

To address those needs, you can add what Apple calls *index links:* hyperlinks from subsequent occurrences of the term for such cases. Follow these steps to add an index link:

1. **Select the term in your text that you want to be the index link.**

   In the Glossary bar, the term appears in the New Glossary Term field because iBooks Author recognizes the term is already in the glossary as a primary glossary link.

2. **In the Index Link For pop-up menu to the right of the New Glossary Term field, choose the glossary term that the newly selected text should be linked to in the glossary.**

3. **Click the adjacent Add Link button.**

   That occurrence of the term now links to the same glossary definition as the original occurrence of the term, but unlike that first occurrence, it doesn't appear in boldface in the text.

The text you select to create the index link doesn't need to be the same as the actually glossary term. Thus, you can create index links from similar terms or variations of the formal term.

After you first add a term to the glossary, search the e-book for every occurrence of that term, adding them to the glossary as index links. That way, you're unlikely to miss any occurrences. Then, go back to that first occurrence and keep reading until you find a new term to be added to the glossary, and repeat the whole process for that new term.

Adding glossary terms' definitions

Adding terms to the glossary isn't helpful if those terms aren't defined. So define the terms; you can do so whenever you want after a term has been added.

To define a term, follow these steps:

1. **Access the glossary term.**

   You can open a glossary's term in several ways:

   - Double-click the Glossary item in the Book panel and select the desired term from the Glossary list, shown in Figure 7-6.

   - Click the » icon button at the far-right of the Glossary bar to open the glossary, then select the desired term from the Glossary pane's list. (The » icon button turns into the « icon button, which you can click to return to where you left off in the e-book.)

   - Click a term in the e-book's text that has been added to the glossary; this brings you right to that term's definition.

   Initially, the term has no definition, so only the term's name appears at the top of the glossary's right pane and some placeholder text appears below the term.

2. **Double-click the placeholder text.**

   That text becomes editable.

3. **Enter your definition.**

   You can provide a simple definition or an encyclopedia-like description, as appropriate for the term and the e-book.

4. **(Optional) Add text boxes, shapes, charts, and tables to the definition by using the same methods you use to add them on your pages and layouts (see Chapter 5).**

   You can't add widgets to a definition.

   Figure 7-6 uses a chart in the definition for BYOD.

5. **(Optional) Drag terms from the Glossary list to the Related Glossary Terms list in the e-book.**

   The Related Glossary Terms list, which appears below the definition, provides a handy way for readers to quickly find related terms.

To get to the glossary on the iPad, the reader taps the TOC icon button (it looks like a three-line bulleted list) when reading the e-book in iBooks, and then she taps the Glossary button that appears.

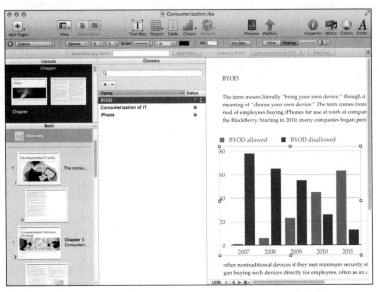

Figure 7-6: Defining a glossary term, with a chart added to the definition.

Editing and removing glossary terms

You can make changes to the glossary terms in several ways:

- ✔ **To edit a glossary term:** Go to the term in the glossary (as described in the preceding section) and double-click the text to edit it.

- ✔ **To remove a term from the Related Glossary Terms section:** Drag it outside the Related Glossary Terms section and then release the pointer.

- ✔ **To delete a term from the glossary:** Select it in the Glossary list and click the – (minus sign) icon button. Doing so deletes the glossary entry, removes the bold formatting from the primary occurrence, and removes the hyperlinks from both the primary occurrences and all index link occurrences.

Finding glossary terms

To find a term in the glossary when the list gets really long, enter the term in the Search bar at the top of the Glossary list, and then press Return.

You may want to find the current term in the e-book itself, such as to understand the context used for the term so that you can better define it in the glossary. In the Index section of the Related Glossary Terms section (below the glossary term's definition), you have two methods available:

- ✔ Click the Find Term button. iBooks Author jumps to the page that contains the primary glossary link to that term. It also opens the Find & Replace panel (see Chapter 3) with the glossary term placed in the Find field so that you can use that panel to find other occurrences of the term in the book, if desired.

- ✔ Below the Find Term button for a glossary entry, a list of all occurrences (the primary glossary link and the index links) of the term in the e-book also appear. Click a reference to jump to that occurrence in the book.

Marking glossary terms

In the Glossary list, the Status column contains blue circular icons. Each of those icons is a pop-up menu that displays two additional circular icons (one green, one yellow). The colors have no intrinsic meaning, and they have no effect on what the reader sees on the iPad. They're meant for your convenience, as a way to mark terms in whatever way is meaningful to you.

For example, you might use color coding to indicate the status of glossary definitions, such as blue for undone, yellow for entered, and green for proofread. Or you might use the colors to indicate up to three categories of terms.

Chapter 8

Publishing and Distributing E-Books

In This Chapter

▶ Making your e-book available outside the iBookstore

▶ Selling or giving away your e-book in the iBookstore

*A*fter you perfect the content and design of your e-book in iBooks Author, you want to have people read it, of course. You can distribute your e-book in two basic ways:

✔ Directly to readers

✔ Via the Apple iBookstore, the e-book portion of its iTunes Store

Apple lets you distribute your e-book outside the iBookstore only if you don't charge money for it. The idea is to let teachers, students, nonprofits, governments, businesses, and anyone give away their e-books to readers for educational purposes.

You can also distribute an iBooks Author e-book for free through the iBookstore, although you need to set up a publishing account with Apple to do so. Those accounts are free to set up and come in two types:

✔ If you have a free publisher account, you can offer only free books in the iBookstore.

✔ If you have a paid account, you can offer both paid and free e-books in the iBookstore. (The account type is called a paid account not because you pay for it, but because it's used to distribute books that readers pay for.)

If you have the paid type of publisher agreement with Apple, you also need an ISBN (International Standard Book Number) for your e-book; its cost varies based on the number purchased and the country in which you reside. You don't need an ISBN if you have a free type of publisher account with Apple.

The bottom line is that to sell an iBooks Author e-book, you *must* distribute it through the iBookstore, which requires an Apple paid publishing account and an ISBN. Apple takes a 30-percent cut of all sales.

Distributing outside the iBookstore

The first step to sharing a free e-book outside the iBookstore is to export the e-book document (an .iba file) to a format that the iPad can read (an .ibooks file). Follow these steps:

1. **Choose File⇨Export.**

   Alternatively, you can choose Share⇨Export. (File is the historic menu for exporting, but with the growth of social media and sharing services, Apple's begun adding a Share menu to its content-creation apps. So you can export from either menu location.)

2. **Go to the iBooks pane in the settings sheet that appears.**

3. **Click Next.**

   The settings sheet changes to one in which you can name the exported file and choose its location (similar to how a typical application's Save As dialog box works).

4. **Enter the filename in the Save As field and select the desired file location from navigation pane below it.**

5. **Click Export to create the .ibooks file.**

After you get the file in the proper format, the next step is to share that file with others. You can make that .ibooks file available in all sorts of ways — the same methods you can use to share any type of file:

✔ As a download link from a website.

✔ As an e-mail attachment (if the size isn't too big).

   You can e-mail an e-book directly from iBooks Author by choosing Share⇨Send via Mail⇨iBook for iPad.

    ✔ From an FTP server.

    ✔ Via CD or DVD.

If recipients get the `.ibooks` file on a Mac or Windows PC, they simply need to drag the file onto the Library section of the Sidebar in iTunes or load it into iTunes by choosing File⇨Add to Library or pressing ⌘+O. When the iPad syncs to the computer, the e-book is transferred to the iPad and available in the iBooks app like any other e-book. If the e-book still doesn't appear in iBooks, follow these steps:

1. **Open iTunes.**

2. **Select the iPad in the Devices section of the iTunes Sidebar.**

3. **Go to the Books pane.**

4. **If it's not already selected, select the Sync Books option.**

5. **Select the All Books option.**

   If the Selected Books check box is selected, select the name of the new e-book in the list of books displayed in the Book pane.

Distributing through the iBookstore

For maximum reach, publish your e-book in Apple's iBookstore. If you don't charge for the e-book, you can both make it available for free in the iBookstore and distribute it for free outside the iBookstore, as described in the preceding section. But if you charge for the e-book, you may distribute it only via the iBookstore.

Setting up a publisher account

To distribute your e-books via the iBookstore, you need to set up a publisher account with Apple. The account is free. To set up the account, go to www.apple.com/itunes/sellcontent in your browser, and then click the Online Application link to open the Create an Account screen in Apple's iTunes Connect service, which is the service used to sell e-books and other content through Apple's various iTunes stores.

You need to choose between a paid account and a free account:

- ✓ **Paid account:** Lets you both sell and give away e-books in the iBookstore
- ✓ **Free account:** Lets you only give away e-books

You can't convert a free account to a paid account later, so if you think you may want to sell e-books at some point, choose the paid account. For a paid account, you need a taxpayer ID for your organization or yourself, as well as the legal name used for a business taxpayer ID, so be sure to get that information before you start.

Also, if you have a developer account with Apple, you can't use that account to sell e-books (or other content) via the iTunes stores. You need a separate account for each type of the iTunes content you intend to distribute (such as e-books, music, and movies). A developer account allows you only to sell iOS and Mac OS X apps through one of Apple's app stores.

After you complete the online application, Apple sends you a confirmation e-mail. For a paid account, the processing can take a few days for Apple to verify your information. After your information is verified, go to iTunes Connect in your browser to set up the remaining details of your account, including agreeing to the account terms. For paid accounts, you can set up additional contacts if you're not an individual or a sole proprietor.

For all paid accounts, you must set up banking information (to deposit your sales receipts) and your taxpayer reporting information (an electronic IRS W-9 form for the U.S., for example).

After your setup is complete, a confirmation screen appears in your browser, such as the one shown in Figure 8-1. In this screen, you download the iTunes Producer software that you need to complete your e-book for distribution in the iBookstore.

You can go to your iTunes Connect account via your browser at any time to view your sales information, download iTunes Producer, and access other related resources by going to `https://itunesconnect.apple.com` and signing in by using the ID and password you established for the account.

Download iTunes Producer to your Mac from the download link at the iTunes Connect welcome page (in Figure 8-1, the link text is iTunes Producer 2.5.1), and then double-click it to run the installer because you need iTunes Producer installed to publish an iBooks Author e-book to the iBookstore.

Figure 8-1: A confirmation screen appears in your browser after you set up a publisher account via iTunes Connect.

Prepping the e-book in iTunes Producer

If you have a paid publisher account with Apple, before you can publish your e-book, you need to get an ISBN for it, even if you're not charging for the book.

You need a separate ISBN for each edition, so if you also plan on publishing a print version, a Kindle version, and/or an ePub version, you need a separate ISBN for each.

To buy an ISBN, go to www.myidentifiers.com if you're in the U.S.; otherwise go to www.isbn-international.org/agency to find your country's ISBN provider.

You don't need an ISBN if you have a free publisher account or if you're distributing an e-book somewhere other than the iBook-store (as described in the "Distributing outside the iBookstore" section, earlier in this chapter). But you can still get an ISBN for e-books published those ways; for example, you might want ISBNs as part of your inventory management system or to prove you're the publisher in case of an ownership dispute.

Exporting the book for iTunes Producer

When your e-book is ready to be published, follow these steps:

1. **Start the export of the book in iBooks Author as an `.itmsp` file by clicking the Publish icon button in the toolbar.**

   Alternatively, you can choose File➪Publish or press Shift+⌘+P.

   The settings sheet shown in Figure 8-2 opens.

   You must use the `.itmsp` file type in iTunes Producer to finalize the e-book for the iBookstore.

2. **Enter a filename in the Save As field.**

3. **Specify a location where you want to save the file in the navigation section of the settings sheet.**

4. **Click Publish to complete the export.**

 The iBookstore has a maximum file size of 2GB for e-books, and Apple recommends keeping e-books less than 1GB in size. It also notes that books larger than 20MB can't be downloaded over cellular (3G and 4G) connections, just over Wi-Fi or via iTunes.

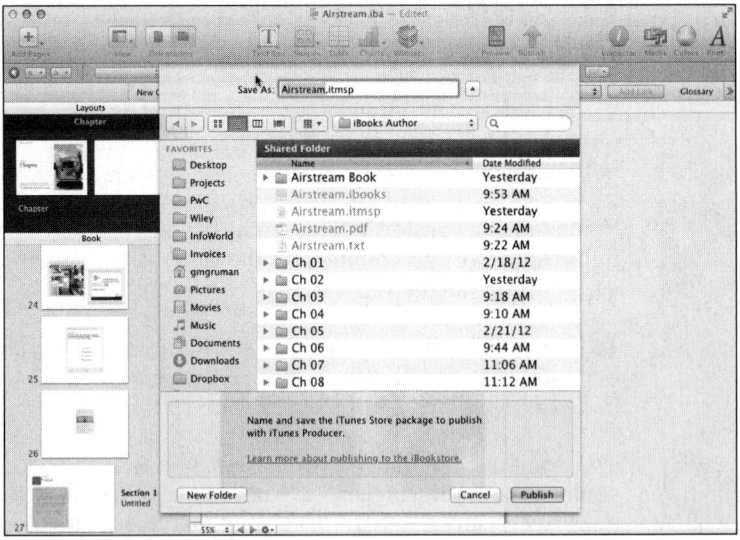

Figure 8-2: Saving an e-book as a .itmsp file for prep in iTunes Producer.

Creating a preview version of your e-book

You must prepare a preview version of your e-book file in iBooks Author so that potential buyers can download it for free to their iPad to see whether they want to get the full edition. In iBooks Author, follow these steps:

1. **Choose File⇨Duplicate to make the copy.**

2. **Remove everything but the portion of the book you want in the preview.**

   For example, you might delete all but the first chapter. Or you might delete all but the first two pages in each chapter. You decide what to provide in the preview.

3. **Choose File⇨Duplicate.**

   A copy of the book document appears in a new window.

4. **Choose File⇨Save.**

   Alternatively, you can press ⌘+S.

   A settings sheet appears.

5. **Enter the filename in the Save As field, use the navigation section to specify the file's location, and click Save to save the file.**

6. **Choose File⇨Export to export the preview version of the book document.**

   Alternatively, you can choose Save⇨Export.

   The settings sheet in which you export the iBooks version (a .ibooks file) of that e-book preview opens.

7. **Click the iBooks icon button, and then click Next.**

8. **In the new settings sheet that appears, enter the filename in the Save As field, use the navigation section to specify the file's location, and then click Export to save the file there.**

   You'll use that preview version of the e-book later in iTunes Producer, so remember where you saved it.

Setting e-book metadata and sales settings

After you export the .itmsp file from iBooks Author (as described in the "Exporting the book for iTunes Producer" section, earlier in this chapter), iTunes Producer opens automatically, displaying the Book pane's Info subpane. Your current iTunes Connect account appears at the upper-right of the iTunes Producer application window; click the account to change it. (iTunes Producer is also used for prepping other types of iTunes store content, and each type requires a separate iTunes Connect account, so you may have more than one account set up.)

Go through each of the subpanes in the Book pane (the buttons are at the bottom of the pane) to set up the required information for the e-book description in the iBookstore. The options are self-explanatory, and if you hover the pointer over a field, a description appears. But do note the following:

✔ **In the Info subpane, you can choose Textbook or Book in the Book Type pop-up menu.** If you choose textbook, your book is categorized in the iBookstore as an educational textbook; if you choose Book, it's considered a regular book.

Also, you must enter a value in the Print Length field, even if you don't intend to create a print edition. Use the page count for the book, which you can get by choosing File➪Print or pressing ⌘+P in iBooks Author; the total page count appears in the settings sheet that opens below the page preview. (Click Cancel to close the settings sheet without printing.)

✔ **In the Rights & Pricing subpane, shown in Figure 8-3, choose Digital Only in the Publication Type pop-up menu if you're not also releasing a printed version.** If you're not releasing a print edition, the price in the Physical List price should match the e-book price chosen in the Price Tier pop-up menu.

Also in this subpane, you can remove the e-book's copy protection individually for each region in which you're distributing the e-book by deselecting its DRM Free option. (Remember that, as Chapter 6 explains, video and audio files in HTML objects aren't protected, regardless of whether you select the DRM Free setting.)

Finally, you must select Cleared for Sale to permit sales in each region.

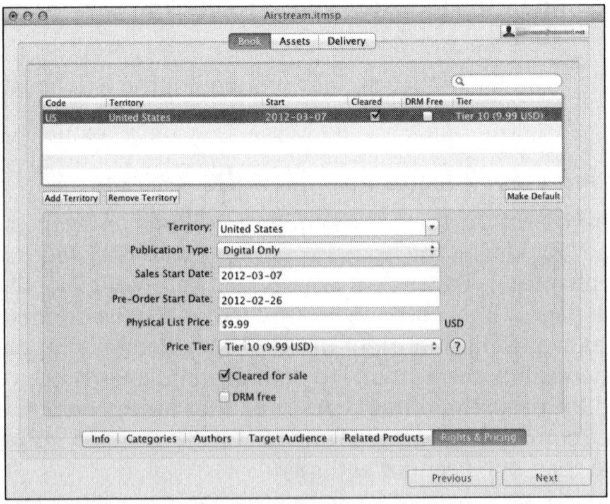

Figure 8-3: The Rights & Pricing subpane in iTunes Producer's Book pane.

Collecting the e-book assets for the iBookstore

When you publish an e-book from iBooks Author, iTunes Producer automatically opens the `.itmsp` file. But you need to submit other files to the iBookstore, in addition to the e-book itself.

You work with the e-book's files in iTunes Producer's Assets pane. Here's what each subpane offers:

- ✔ **Publication:** Update the iBooks Author e-book by clicking Choose below the Upload Publication area to load a different document file (or, more likely, an updated version of it). In the Open dialog box that appears, navigate to the updated `.itmsp` file and click Open.

  Click the Choose button below the Upload Publication Preview area to upload the preview version of the e-book you created (as explained in the section "Creating a preview version of your e-book," earlier in this chapter). In the Open dialog box that appears, navigate to the preview book's `.ibooks` file and click Open.

- ✔ **Cover Art:** The cover set in the Book Title page in iBooks Author appears (see Chapter 2). If you want to replace this cover with a different image, click Choose, and then select the desired replacement cover image from your Mac in the Open dialog box that appears and click Open.

- ✔ **Screenshots:** Add images of your book's pages (these images will appear in the iBookstore's page for your e-book). To create a screenshot of selected pages, preview the e-book on the iPad (as Chapter 2 explains), and then press the Home button and the Wake/Sleep button simultaneously to take a screenshot. Then, transfer the images from the iPad's Photos app to your Mac via iTunes, iPhoto, iCloud, Wi-Fi beaming (in iOS 5.1 or later), or e-mail.

You can save the e-book in iTunes Producer, so you don't have to complete everything in one sitting. Just choose File➪Save or press ⌘+S. When you're ready to continue working on the e-book, launch iTunes Producer and open the `.itmsp` file: Choose File➪Open or press ⌘+O, and then locate the file in the Open dialog box and click Open. Alternatively, you can choose File➪Open Recent and choose the file from the submenu of recent files that appears.

Submitting the e-book for distribution in the iBookstore

When you finish prepping the book and its elements in iTunes Producer, it's time to submit the submit the book to the Apple iBookstore. Follow these steps:

1. **Go to the Delivery pane.**

   The Delivery pane in iTunes Producer lists any issues that must be addressed before you can submit the e-book to the iBookstore.

2. **Go to the appropriate panes and subpanes to resolve any issues listed.**

   iTunes Producer lists the fields or other items that need to be corrected, but not which pane or subpane they reside in, so you may have to hunt for the settings to correct.

3. **After you resolve all the issues, save the .itmsp file by choosing File⇨Save.**

   Alternatively, you can press ⌘+S.

4. **Make sure you have an active Internet connection for your Mac.**

5. **Click Deliver in the Delivery pane.**

   Alternatively, you can choose File⇨Save and Deliver or press ⌘+D.

   If you have multiple e-books ready to be uploaded to Apple, choose File⇨Save and Deliver All or press Shift+⌘+D.

   At this point, iTunes Producer uploads the e-book to Apple's servers. (If you see an error message saying the files aren't saved, don't panic. iTunes Producer itself should save the files and continue the upload process.) The upload could take several minutes, depending on the speed of your Internet connection, the size of your e-book file, and how busy Apple's iTunes Connect servers are.

6. **Go to your iTunes Connect account via your web browser to verify that everything is as you expected.**

   You can see the status of your e-books by clicking the Manage Your Books link in iTunes Connect.

Index